Creating an Inclusive School

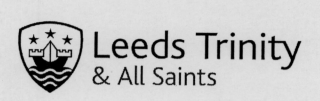

Also available from Continuum

Behaviour Management, Tony Swainston

Creative Assemblies, Brian Radcliff

Effective Learning, Gavin Reid and Shannon Green

Emotional Literacy, David Spendlove

Encouraging Reading, Susan Elkin

Putting Assessment for Learning into Practice, David Spendlove

Tacking Bullying in Schools, Daniel Guiney

Teaching NLP in the Classroom, Kate Spohrer

Available from Network

Inclusion in Schools: Making a Difference, Rosemary Sage

Creating an Inclusive School

Mal Leicester

Ideas in Action

continuum

Continuum International Publishing Group

The Tower Building
11 York Road
London, SE1 7NX

80 Maiden Lane, Suite 704
New York,
NY 10038

www.continuumbooks.com

© Mal Leicester 2008

British Library Cataloguing-in-Publication Data
A catalogue record for this book is available from the British Library.

ISBN: 9781855394544 (paperback)

Library of Congress Cataloging-in-Publication Data
A catalog record for this book is available from the Library of Congress.

Typeset by
Bookens Ltd, Royston, Herts
Printed and bound in Great Britain by
MPG Books, Cornwall
Illustrations by Martin Aston

To my late father, Eddie Leicester,
with love, respect and thanks

Contents

Acknowledgements ix
Introduction xi

Chapter 1 – *What* is inclusion? 2
What is inclusion? 2
Exclusion and prejudice 4
Exclusion and discrimination 6
Bullying and self-confidence 8
Name-calling and bullying 10
Education for all: Equal opportunities 12

Chapter 2 – *Who* is excluded? 14
In-groups and out-groups 14
Special needs: Disability awareness 16
Special needs: Warnock and integration 18
Multicultural education: In rural schools 20
Multicultural education: In city schools 22
Education and gender 24
Family background 26

Chapter 3 – *Why* is inclusion important? 28
The damage from exclusion 28
Inclusive learning and values 30
Justice and care 32
Making changes, removing barriers and promoting respect 34

Chapter 4 – The *how* of inclusion: Curriculum and resources 36
Curriculum development and inclusion 36
Inclusion in the curriculum 38
Bias in learning resources 40
Positive learning resources 42
Early years: Inclusive learning in the six domains 44
Inclusive learning at Key Stages 1 and 2: 7–11 46
Inclusive learning at Key Stages 3 and 4: 11–14 48
Beyond school: Inclusive education 15+ 50

Chapter 5 – The *how* of inclusion: Inclusion in the classroom   52

An inclusive pedagogy   52

Classroom ethos   54

Inclusive practice: The value of circle time (4–11)   56

Inclusive practice: The power of story (4–11)   58

Inclusive practice: The secondary school   60

Inclusion in the playground   62

Chapter 6 – A whole-school approach   64

Inclusion: The legal context 1   64

Inclusion: The legal context 2   66

The school ethos   68

The school assembly   70

The head or senior management   72

Staffing and inclusion   74

Parents and inclusion   76

School governors and inclusion   78

Five key governor duties and inclusion   80

Continuing professional development and inclusion   82

Raising awareness: Training for inclusion   84

Further reading   87

Acknowledgments

I would like to thank Angela Perrin for typing the manuscript with competence and good humour and Roger Twelvetrees for invaluable encouragement and support. My daughter Jane Dover has helped me to understand the pervasiveness of the exclusion of disabled people and my work at AFFOR informed my understanding of the subtlety and institutionalisation of racism.

Introduction

Good teachers want to create a supportive classroom and to see *all* their pupils develop and flourish. This book will help such teachers to achieve their goals by explaining how and why prejudice, discrimination and bullying can damage children's learning. It will show teachers how to develop an *inclusive* practice in the classroom, the curriculum and the playground. It is only when inclusive practice permeates the full range of each child's school experiences that children from all backgrounds and of all abilities and disabilities will become happy and effective learners. In addition, the book will encourage a whole-school approach to inclusion by suggesting strategies for creating a school that is caring, disciplined and fair.

Chapters 1 and 2 cover the *what* and *who* of inclusion. We will explore *what* is meant by 'inclusion' and see *why* it involves countering endemic social stereotypes and prejudices and also bullying behaviours such as name-calling, scape-goating and intimidation. We will also consider which children are most vulnerable to exclusion and to bullying. Attention is given to ethnicity and multicultural education, and to special needs and the inclusion of children with a variety of impairments. Gender issues and family background will also be addressed. We will begin to explore how to be positive about 'difference' – in short, how to welcome and flourish in *diversity*.

Chapter 3 focuses on why inclusion is important. Each child, regardless of gender, ethnicity, disability, sexuality or family background should have the opportunity to fulfil their educational potential. Without inclusive practice, some children will be hindered in their learning; they will experience alienation; they will be unhappy in school and experience a loss of self-esteem.

Chapter 4 looks at inclusion in the curriculum and in resources, and Chapter 5 at inclusion in classroom practice. Each of these chapters explains general principles and also gives advice, specifically and in practical terms, about what inclusion requires at the various ages and stages of education – from the early years through to young adulthood.

Finally, all this discussion and guidance is brought together in Chapter 6, which considers a 'whole-school' approach to inclusion. Education rests on inclusive values but how do we foster these? How do we develop a whole-school approach to inclusion? How do we develop an inclusive school policy? What would this contain? How do we create an inclusive school ethos and a positive visual environment? What are the implications of inclusion for teaching and other staff, for parents, for governors and for continuing professional development?

It is easy to think that teachers have enough to do in covering the National Curriculum without bothering about inclusion. Teachers are busy people. However, the National Curriculum itself requires schools to have regard to the development of personal, social, moral, emotional, cultural and spiritual values. In any case, unhappy children do not learn well and will not learn to love learning or learn how to learn.

The issues around inclusion are too important to neglect. The values upon which it is built are the values of a good education because a good education requires 'effective' learning *and* will be morally 'good' too – i.e. fair and humane for every member of the school community.

What is inclusion?

What is inclusion?

The Chambers Dictionary defines 'inclusion' as 'the act of including', with 'includes' given as 'to enclose'. In the school context, the emphasis on 'act' is appropriate because to ensure that all the children feel they belong, and to ensure that no child meets preventable barriers to learning, does indeed require positive action on the part of teachers – indeed of the whole-school community. Moreover, to genuinely 'be comprised as a part' of that community requires that the child feels at home there. This entails that unless there is a sound educational reason, we do not expect a child to have to change fundamental aspects of their identity – such as aspects of cultural background – in order to conform to the school. Rather, the school seeks to change itself in order to sensitively enclose the child. This often requires a re-orientation in our thinking.

To turn now to 'exclusion'. The Chambers gives several definitions: 'to shut out', 'to prevent from entering', 'to omit', 'to prevent from taking part' and 'to leave out'. In the school context 'to shut out or prevent from entering' may be physical (wheelchair access issues or some kinds of entry requirements) or psychological (allowing the child to 'feel different': bullying). 'To omit' reminds us that we can exclude unintentionally (allowed into the school but subsequently feeling alienated) – for example, by not having multicultural learning resources or resources suitable for a partially sighted child. 'Awareness' precedes 'action' and this kind of understanding should become part of our professional knowledge.

Advice

The meaning of inclusion is itself inclusive! It links with countering prejudice, discrimination, and bullying, having concern for all vulnerable children. It values equal opportunities in education

Key points

- Inclusion, applied to schools, has far-reaching implications.

- Since the Warnock Report (1988) advocated integration of disabled children into mainstream schools, inclusion tends to be associated with disability. However, the concept embraces the whole-school population.

- The Warnock Report: Warnock, M. (1988), *Report of the Committee of Enquiry into the Education of Handicapped Children and Young People* (London: HMSO).

A starting point

- As a starting point to the actions and changes recommended throughout this book, consider what you already have in place. For example:

  - A SENCO (How much support do they receive? Should it be more?).
  - Multicultural resources. (Are these adequate? Do they permeate classroom resources, library provision, the visual environment, e.g. pictures on the walls, etc.?)
  - A policy on equal opportunities. (If this does not exist consider setting up a working party to develop one.)
  - A policy/guidelines on bullying. (If this does not exist consider setting up a working party to develop one.)
  - What else do you already have in place and how could this be further developed?

Application

Exclusion and prejudice

Prejudice is learned. Research has shown that even very young children acquire the prejudices of the wider society. Prejudice is a preconceived opinion or bias for or against someone or something where the opinion has been formed without adequate information on which to make a rational judgement. It goes beyond a simple pre-judgement however, in that there is some emotional investment in these irrational beliefs. There is emotional resistance to changing such beliefs in the light of new evidence. Indeed, evidence is distorted to fit in with prejudice. Moreover, as studies have shown, prejudice is expressed in harmful discriminatory behaviour.

Widely shared prejudices find expression in stereotypes, which distort our perceptions of individuals from the stereotyped group. These stereotypes are reinforced by the media and by mis-educative books and even wrong assumptions in lessons in schools. But media studies can be a useful means of teaching children about stereotyping and bias and developing their critical faculties about group oppression.

Prejudice is expressed in discriminatory behaviour and if a group receives sufficient discrimination they become a disadvantaged group in many ways. The more powerful and privileged groups blame the victim. In other words, the disadvantage experienced by these groups because of discrimination by the more powerful is then blamed on the groups themselves. They are said to be poor because they are lazy; unemployed because lacking in skill; harassed by the police because more criminal, etc. Thus prejudice and discrimination reinforce each other in a vicious circle, and the oppressor is able to find justification for his or her discriminatory treatment of the disfavoured, less powerful, vulnerable groups.

Prejudice is also expressed in the language we use, which is why words can wound. Teachers need to develop a sensitivity to acceptable/unacceptable terminology and to changes in this.

- Common stereotypes of disabled children include:

    - Pitiable/noble
    - Evil
    - Freak
    - Burden
    - Incapable.

- Common stereotypes of minority ethnic group children include:

    - Lazy
    - Aggressive
    - Volatile
    - Good at sport and music
    - Poor at academic work.

- Common stereotype of girls include:

    - Passive/unadventurous
    - Vain/empty-headed
    - Victims
    - Weak
    - Nurturing/home-lovers.

- Examples of unacceptable terms include:

    - Cripple, handicapped, subnormal, a 'special needs' child.
    - Coloured, half-caste, an 'ethnic' child.
    - Bird, Sheila, bitch, the term 'girl' when used of a woman.
    - Pansy, pufter (and other derogatory terms used for gay people).

- Seminal works on prejudice include:

    - Allport, W. H. (1958), *Prejudice* (New York: Doubleday).
    - Milner, D. (1983), *Children and Race Ten Years On* (London: Ward Lock).

Application

Exclusion and discrimination

We have seen that prejudice, when widespread in the dominant group, can lead to discrimination against minorities. The Swann Report recognized that discrimination may go beyond prejudiced *individuals* who discriminate against members of a group they dislike. Discrimination can become built into the way institutions function. It defined institutional discrimination as:

> 'The way in which a range of long established systems, practices and procedures in education and the wider society, which were originally devised to meet the needs of a relatively homogeneous society, may unintentionally work against minority groups by depriving them of opportunities open to the majority population.'

The significant point about this conception is that it draws attention to structures and processes within institutions that are harmful in their effect. It is *outcome* rather than *intention* that is important.

Thus discrimination can be both individual and institutional. It can also be deliberate or unintentional. In other words, a person (an individual) might deliberately behave unfairly or might do so unwittingly. An institution, too, might be deliberate in its discriminations or, more often with schools, unaware of how its established ways of doing things might disadvantage some groups of children.

Similarly, as the Race Relations Act recognizes, deliberate discrimination may be direct or indirect.

Direct discrimination occurs when a person is treated less favourably on grounds of race or gender than a person of another race or gender would be in the same, or not materially different, circumstances.

Indirect discrimination takes place when a requirement or condition, applied equally to all races or both sexes, to the able bodied and the disabled, has the effect in practice of excluding a considerably greater proportion of one group than another.

Advice

Individual and institutional discrimination

- Individual discrimination. An example – for a manager to deliberately choose a less worthy candidate over one from a disfavoured group.

- Institutional discrimination – an interview process that has no checks and balances for such unfair behaviour, such as: a representative group for the short listing, representative interview panel members, a person specification, a job specification, the take-up of all references, similar procedures and questions for all candidates.

Deliberate and unintentional discrimination

- Deliberate discrimination is less common in schools than in many other places since most teachers want to be fair to all their pupils.

- Unintentional discrimination may occur, for example:
  - Letters home only in English to non-English-speaking parents.
  - Some uniform requirements may be difficult for cultural reasons or because of the expense involved.
  - As teachers we may automatically ask for an essay about Christmas, rather than allowing a choice of celebration.

Direct and indirect discrimination

- Direct discrimination is any requirement that unfairly excludes – such as not allowing a disabled person to apply even when their impairment is not relevant.

- Examples of indirect discrimination include – word of mouth recruitment excluding black applicants for a job if the networks and circles of people passing on the information are all white; or a requirement for a qualification (say English GCSE) where this is not relevant to the job, and tends to disqualify some ethnic minority groups.

Application

7

Bullying and self-confidence

Children should approach other children with interest and friendship rather than with fear and fighting. Children often bully and get bullied if they feel insecure. Therefore, part of the move to counter bullying must be to build each child's self-confidence; to help each child feel good about himself or herself and to be able to express what they want or need or feel.

Most people have bullied someone at least once. However, bullies pick on people all the time because it makes them feel good. They have a problem. With the children's help you can make a list of reasons why people become bullies. For example: they are being bullied themselves; they are spoilt and always want their own way; they are sad or frustrated and want others to feel bad too; they are scared they might get bullied unless they seem tough; they are jealous of people who have more or seem happier.

With the children's help you could also make a list of things a bully could do to stop being a bully. For example: tell an adult you trust; make friends with a new pupil and help them; say sorry to someone who they have bullied; give themselves a fresh start with new people by joining a club; refuse to be part of a bullying gang.

Finally, give the children strategies with which to deal with bullying should it happen to them. For example, how to deal with insults or name-calling, how to say 'no', and the importance of telling an adult when bullying is repeated or serious.

A school must do all it can to prevent bullying occurring and be vigilant to the possibility. Children who claim that they are being bullied must be listened to and supported. In primary schools you can use circle time to build self-confidence and to discuss bullying and what you can do about it. Some secondary schools have found ways to involve the children themselves in countering bullying. For example, they have set up pupil mentoring systems and support committees.

Advice

Assertiveness exercises

- Ask the children to make a list of things they are good at, things they like about themselves and good things that they have done.

- Help children to make friends. Give them some indications of what to do: to show an interest, to smile, to laugh at jokes, to say something nice, to pay a genuine compliment.

- And what not to do: not to be insulting, not to be bossy, not to talk only about yourself, not only to do the things that you want to do.

- You can also have sessions about dealing with insults: ignore the insult as if you don't care, make a joke in response, just smile and carry on with what you are doing, walk away.

- It's also important that children learn how to say no. Give them some helpful ideas of positive ways of saying no, with examples such as:

  'Can I copy your work?'
  'No, the teacher can tell and we'll both be in trouble.'

  'Can I borrow your trainers?'
  'No, sorry.'

  'Lend me some money?'
  'No, I only have my dinner money.'

  'Give me some sweets.'
  'Sorry, they're all gone.'

  'You've pinched my book. Can I look in your bag?'
  'No, I haven't. Get the teacher to check.'

You could give the children some address and telephone numbers that might be helpful. For example: Kidsafe, 152 Buckingham Palace Road, London SW1W 9TR, telephone 020 7730 3300 Monday to Friday 10am – 4pm. Kidsafe offers helpful advice to children who are being bullied.

Free helplines don't show up on the telephone bill:
Childline 0800 1111, Samaritans 0345 909090.

Name-calling and bullying

Many children experience name-calling and other forms of bullying. It is important that all teachers seek to establish a non-bullying culture in their classroom and in the children's school world. Your own example of non-bullying is important – as is how you deal with bullying; taking it seriously and having a consistent policy about it. Adults need to be sensitive to children's experiences of bullying and to recognize that name-calling is not harmless – but the start of bullying behaviour. The children too need to learn that name-calling and other forms of bullying are wrong, and what to do about these.

As children and even as adults we are all potential victims of bullying. (The incidence of bullying at work is surprisingly high.) The perception of someone being different is often the trigger for bullying behaviour. A good education teaches children to be interested in rather than threatened by difference. If children un-learn social prejudices against social minorities this will tend to reduce bullying.

Bullying is cowardly because the person picks on someone weaker or smaller who can't fight back. They pick on people's differences because they have never understood that we are all different and this makes getting to know people more interesting. It saddens me that I was unaware, at the time, of the bullying that my disabled daughter experienced in her first school – the only mainstream school that she attended. I wish that I had explained to her that if you are bullied it is not your fault and told her very clearly that I would always help if it happened to her.

Even with young children teachers are not always aware that bullying is happening. Parents and teachers must seek to create an anti-bullying ethos, be vigilant and always listen sympathetically to a child who perceives him or herself to be either bullying or bullied, and subsequently to do something to change the situation.

Teachers can also provide children with ways of dealing with name-calling. For example: ignore the name-calling as though you don't care and the bully may get bored; walk away; tell an adult whom you trust.

Advice

Anti-bullying resources

Classroom resources:

- Goldthorpe, M. (2001), 'Who's A Bully?', in *Poems for Circle Time and Literacy Hour* (Wisbech: LDA). (This contains other useful poems and material relevant to bullying.)
- Leicester, M. and Johnson, G. (2004), *Stories for Inclusive Schools. Developing Young Pupils' Skills* (London: Routeledge Falmer).
- Leicester, M. (2007), *Special Stories for Disability Awareness. Stories and Activities for Teachers, Parents and Professionals* (London: Jessica Kingsley).
- Moseley, J. (1996), *Helping Children Deal with Bullying, Anger and Conflict* (Wisbech: LDA).

Resources for schools and teachers:

- Rigby, K. (2002), *Stop The Bullying: A Handbook for Schools* (London: Jessica Kingsley).
- Baker, K. and Smith, B. (2006), *Making a Spectacle of Bullying* (London: Sage).
- Dubin, N. (2006), *Being Bullied: Strategies and Solutions for People with Asperger's Syndrome* (London: Jessica Kingsley).
- Moseley, J. (1996), *Working Towards a Whole School Policy on Self-Esteem and Positive Behaviour* (Wisbech: LDA).

A 'No Bullying Here' poster

- Primary school: write 'No Bullying Here' at the top of a poster-sized sheet. Give each child a plain postcard and have them paint a beautiful object on it. These can be stuck round the poster to make a colourful frame. Now, with the children's help, write down suggestions about how to stop bullying, until the poster is filled.
- Secondary school: involve the children in constructing an anti-bullying policy for the school (aims, procedures, advice, monitoring, etc.).

Application

Education for all: Equal opportunities

The movement for equal opportunities and LEA Equal Opportunity Policy Statements, the EO Literature and EO Legislation are, like a commitment to inclusion, concerned with fair, equitable treatment for everyone, regardless of social background. However, fair and equal treatment is not equivalent to treating everyone the same. We are all different and have different interest and needs. For example, it is clearly not fair to provide the same reading materials (standard size print books) to blind or partially sighted children as to the sighted.

In general, however, there is much similarity between promoting equal opportunities and promoting inclusion. There is perhaps a difference in emphasis. 'Equal opportunities' tends to focus on group inequality and political solutions. 'Inclusion' tends to focus on the individual learner, including the inclusion of vulnerable children who are not necessarily members of one of the socially disadvantaged groups.

Equal opportunities have been seen to cover at least four ideas:

1   A basic conception of equal opportunities; to promote policies and practices that eliminate or avoid some of the current direct and indirect unfair discrimination in education. Fairness is not always about same treatment or equal distribution. To treat people equally means treating them equally well and this often means not treating them the same. Equal medical treatment would not entail the same quantity of drugs for each patient but would entail equally good medical care for each one.

2   A substantive conception of equal opportunities; to promote policies and practices that would lead to greater ability and motivation in those who currently have relatively less.

3   A liberal conception of equal opportunities; to promote the development of respect for all people.

4   A radical conception of equal opportunities; to promote equality for social groups as social groups, for example, through the use of quota systems.

Advice

The application of equal opportunities has two dimensions:

● A general application

Teachers should ensure that every pupil is educated against widely shared prejudices. We mis-educate if we pass on stereotypes. And does the History curriculum enable pupils to understand the roots of racism? Does the school's cross-curricular values education show pupils that there is not just one proper way of life – of dress, or worship, or cuisine, or music and so on?

● A special application

The school should ensure that the needs and interests of pupils from disadvantaged groups are not neglected relative to mainstream needs and interests. For example: do school dinners cater for all groups? Does the school's religious education cater for all local faith groups?

The application of equal opportunities applies to staff issues too:

● Does the school's staff, teaching and non-teaching, represent a diversity of background?

● Are women, black and disabled teachers clustered at the lower grades?

● Does the teaching staff have sufficient expertise in equal opportunity issues?

● Do you use word of mouth recruitment? This tends to discriminate against minority ethnic groups.

● Consider stating in your advertisement that you are an equal opportunity employer.

● Do not ask female candidates about family responsibilities. Family and family planning are their own business!

There is a huge amount of literature on equal opportunities in education including handbooks, reports and guidelines from government (DfES), local education authorities and statutory and voluntary organizations. Books include comprehensive approaches about equal opportunities in general and there are also books that focus on particular aspects, such as minority ethnic groups, girls/women, social class or disabled children, or dealing with homophobia in secondary schools where pupils may be discovering that they are gay.

Application

Who is excluded?

In-groups and out-groups

Children from some social groups are particularly vulnerable. They may experience exclusion because of the prejudice against their particular group: their class, or race, or culture, or disability, or sexuality or gender. Creating an inclusive school involves ensuring that no person is treated less favourably than any other, for no other reason than his or her social class, sexual orientation, colour and culture, gender or disabilities.

In our society, members of minority ethnic groups (particularly black groups), people with some disabilities, homosexual people and women, meet with prejudice and discrimination, to the point of serious disadvantage, in education and in other crucial areas of their lives. For example, non-English-speaking parents may receive letters from school only in English, and young women teachers may be refused posts because governors assume that they plan to start a family. For a particular individual this prejudice and discrimination may oppress them from more than one direction. For example, they may be black and a woman. Of course there are limits to how far education can affect entrenched social attitudes and structures. Nevertheless, we are not born with prejudiced attitudes. Prejudice is learned. Since education is about individual learning and development, schools have a role to play.

It's because this anti-stereotyping education is so important that the Swann Committee, charged by the government to investigate the education of ethnic minority children, entitled their report *Education for All* (Swan 1986). The prevalence of prejudice and discrimination against minority groups has educational implications for us all.

Advice

- The Swann Report, entitled *Education For All* is an important but very long report. The Swann Report (1985) Great Britain, Department for Education and Science (London: HMSO).
- The Runnymede Trust produced a concise summary.
- Children from out-groups who may be particularly vulnerable include:
  - Poor children.
  - Minority ethnic group children, particularly black children.
  - 'Mixed race' children.
  - Disabled children.
  - Gay (teenage children).
  - Gender can also disadvantage girls in some situations and boys in others.
- Some children who are not from these 'out-groups' may feel 'different' and may be bullied. They include:
  - Children whose appearance may attract adverse attention (glasses, red hair, obesity or whatever).
  - Children whose parents or carers are different in appearance or lifestyle (e.g. the children of travellers).
  - Shy children who may lack social skills.
  - Children who stutter.

Application

Special needs: Disability awareness

We all have a range of abilities and disabilities. We label people as disabled if their disability is sufficiently handicapping. Yet, the degree to which a disability is a handicap depends upon the social context within which we function. Being unable to walk is a handicap if schools, theatres, etc., fail to provide wheelchair access. Being unable to see is a handicap if letters, books and newspapers are not provided in Braille. Alternative teaching approaches can often overcome a pupil's learning difficulties and, if particular skills cannot be mastered, social structures determine the degree to which lack of these will be penalised in terms of employment, income, status and damaged self-esteem. Disability awareness means adopting this perspective on disability, and is often referred to as the social model. Schools with this perspective try to give people their rights rather than acting out of pity. It leads to increased recognition of disablist language and assumptions, to empowerment rather than patronization. This awareness should permeate the education of all children in mainstream schools. Their attitude affects the children with special needs in their own schools and in the wider society.

The barriers experienced by disabled children affect their whole family. Parents of special children have understandable extra anxieties and often carry irrational feelings of guilt. Siblings too have to come to terms with the situation (for example, the extra parental attention their brother or sister requires) and should not be expected to assume responsibility for their disabled sister or brother at school.

There are positive and negative perspectives on disability. A good starting point is to move away from negative perspectives which see disability as illness or tragedy and which generate pity rather than genuine recognition of rights and equality. This model of disability, which locates disability with the individual person, has been called the medical model. It is contrasted with the much more positive social model, which locates disability in a restricting environment. This perspective underlines the disability rights movement.

Disability awareness

School Environment:

We see the importance of environmental factors in schools too. A blind child can gain from the provision of Braille, a partially sighted child from large print books. Some children will suffer from the imposition of inflexible and insensitive school uniform. A deaf child may need a signing support worker.

Further reading for teachers:

- Hull, J. (1992), *Touching the Rock: An Experience of Blindness* (London: Vintage).
- Leicester, M. (1998), *Disability Voice. Towards an Enabling Education* (London: Jessica Kingsley).
- Swain, J. *et al.* (eds) (2002), *Disabling Barriers, Enabling Environments* (London: Sage).

Bibliographies:

- *Children's Literature and Disability* (2001) compiled by the National Information Centre for Children and Youth with Disabilities (NICHCY) (now the National Dissemination Centre for Children with Disabilities) lists children's books featuring individuals with disabilities. This resource is available on the Web at www/nichcy.org/pubs/bibliog./bib5txt.htm
- *Guide for Reviewing Children's Literature that Include People with Disabilities: Books Written for Children Three to Five Years of Age* (2002) compiled by Diane Nastir, Circle of Inclusion Project, provides teachers with information about how to evaluate children's literature that include people with disabilities. It is specifically targeted for general and special education teachers of pre-school-aged children. This resource is available at the Web at www. circleofinclusion.org/english/books/index.html

Special needs: Warnock and integration

In 1978 the Warnock report proposed that most pupils currently in special schools should be integrated into ordinary schools and this was given legal force by the Education Act 1981. Special schools would educate the smaller proportion of pupils with severe or complex disabilities, and should strengthen their links with ordinary schools, offering short-term provision, providing specialist expertise and acting as resource centres.

The report defines special needs in terms of learning difficulties that call for special educational provision. The report sought to remove schools from rigid and harmful categorization to more useful and more positive descriptions: not *mentally* or *physically handicapped*, or *educationally subnormal*, but having *learning difficulties*, which might be mild, moderate or severe.

At the moment many children experience an educational and social apartheid, being bussed away from their home area and thus becoming isolated from peers in their neighbourhood. For these children, integration means the absence of social isolation, social acceptance instead, and being treated the same as everyone else. The Warnock Report describes integration as the central contemporary issue in special education, and as an international conviction that as far as humanely possible the disabled should share the opportunities offered to the non-disabled. It is called mainstreaming in the USA and normalization in Scandinavia and Canada. In Sweden almost all children with special needs have been integrated for some time.

This kind of inclusion, however, will only work if the 'education for all' dimension of promoting inclusion is not neglected. All pupils in the school should develop a disability awareness perspective. The Warnock Report captured this wider need for changed attitudes to disability. This represents an educational gain for all pupils. Inclusion is thus a potential benefit in the moral education of the whole school population.

Advice

- Learning difficulties are defined as requiring one or more of the following:
  - The provision of special needs access to the curriculum through special equipment, facilities or resources, modification of the physical environment, or specialist teaching techniques.
  - The provision of a special or modified curriculum.
  - Particular attention to the social structure and emotional climate in which education takes place.

- The conditions leading to such special educational needs cover a wide range including:
  - physical disability
  - sensory impairment
  - low ability
  - delicate
  - epileptic
  - gifted
  - emotionally disturbed.

- The report also pointed out that integration will only work if certain conditions are fulfilled. These conditions are:
  - that there should be planned entry;
  - support from the governing body;
  - a designated specialist teacher;
  - a school-based resource centre;
  - a limit to the proportion of these children;
  - a planning framework by the LEA;
  - in short, successful inclusion of disabled children requires careful planning, adequate support and in-service training for the teachers.

- Integration is a process, not a single event. First comes planning, then a phased entry into the ordinary school. For some children, staying in a special school but attending an ordinary school for social and some educational activities may be the best option. For other children full phasing into the ordinary school may be the aim.

Application

Multicultural education: In rural schools

Britain is a multiracial and multicultural society. Sadly, prejudice and discrimination adversely affect the lives of black children and their families. Deep prejudice is a particular problem for white schools where racist assumptions are prevalent but people are unaware of these prejudices, stereotypes and omissions. In schools the children may learn from biased books and learning materials. Many books simply omit any reference to black people or minority cultures and may contain stereotyped images, incorrect information and negative attitudes and assumptions. Most are written by white authors and reflect white middle-class virtues and lifestyles as the norm. We have learned these prejudiced assumptions and stereotypes and will need to recognize and overcome our own biased assumptions and prejudiced attitudes.

We must recognize that though different ethnic groups have different traditions (do some things in different ways) there is no one correct way. No ethnic group, including the majority ethnic group, has a monopoly on truth or virtue.

It is in the rural schools that progress in multicultural education has often been slowest and yet in some ways multicultural education is even more important in these white schools. Racial prejudices, stereotyping and myths may flourish in areas where white people do not mix with black people and do not know them as friends.

In many schools, nothing in the visual environment (the posters, artefacts or drawings) or in the curriculum, even indicate that black people exist. For their knowledge of black people in minority cultures, children are left to the mercy of the British media. Studies have established that from an early age, white children are developing negative racial attitudes (Milner, D. (1983), *Children and Race Ten Years On* (London: Ward Lock)).

All schools, including white schools, should have multicultural learning resources and a multicultural curriculum and should deal with racial abuse as a serious part of bullying.

Advice

20

Examples of books for children: Pre-school:

- Weiss, G. D. and Thiele, B. (1995), *What a Wonderful World* (London: Atheneum).
- Thomas, J. C. (1999), *You Are My Perfect Baby* (London: Harper Collins).
- Leicester, M. (2007), *Early Years Stories for the Foundation Stage* (London: Routledge).

Examples of books for children: Primary:

- Hausherr, R. (1997), *Celebrating Families* (London: Scholastic).
- Delacre, L. (1996), *Golden Tales: Myths, Legends and Folktales from Latin America* (London: Scholastic).
- Bridges, R. (1999), *Through My Eyes* (London: Scholastic).

Reading for teachers:

- Fryer, P. (1984), *Staying Power: History of Black People in Britain* (London: Pluto Press).
- Gaine, C. (1987), *No Problem Here: A Practical Approach to Education and 'Race' in White Schools* (London: Hutchinson).

Application

Multicultural education: In city schools

In multicultural inner-city schools the needs of children whose first language is not English need to be considered. It is also good if there is a multicultural, multi-ethnic staff so that children have role models in the teachers who teach them. Good multicultural schools will work closely in partnership with parents and some have home–school liaison teachers.

Racist abuse, harassment and graffiti should never be ignored. In primary schools, very young children using racial abuse require educative rather than punitive response, but in secondary schools, racist incidents should be recognized as a disciplinary matter.

Governors, in consultation with teachers and parents, should develop school procedures for dealing with racist incidents. Such procedures will need to cover a range of situations and in serious cases parents of the abuser and abused should be involved. Some local education authorities have produced guidelines for schools about dealing with racial incidents and these may be helpful.

It is essential that the children receive a multicultural curriculum and that school and classroom resources reflect our multicultural society.

In a multi-ethnic school regard must also be paid to providing food that all the children can eat, whatever their religious or cultural background. A range of choices, drawing on cultural variety and including vegetarian options, will mean that all pupils can receive an enjoyable and nutritious lunch.

Finally, multi-ethnic schools will need to consider their school assembly and religious education. Legal requirements leave scope for multfaith approaches, through which children learn about and respect various world faiths and think about the nature of religion and religious values.

Examples of books for children: Pre-school:

- Tarpley, N. A. (1998), *I Love My Hair!* (London: Little, Brown).
- Heo, Y. (1994), *One Afternoon* (London: Orchard).

Examples of books for children: Primary:

- Pinkney, S. L. (2000), *Shades of Black: A Celebration of Our Children* (London: Scholastic).
- King, C. and Barret, L. (1997), *Oh, Freedom! Kids Talk About the Civil Rights Movement with the People Who Made it Happen* (London: Knopf).
- Taylor, M. D. (1999), *Roll of Thunder, Hear My Cry* (London: Scholastic).

Dealing with racial abuse

- Teachers, non-teaching staff, pupils and parents should know that racial abuse is not acceptable and will not be ignored.
- Abuse is never justified. Even when responding to provocation by a black child, racism is not an acceptable form of response. Conversely a black child reacting to racial abuse may react inappropriately (for example, with physical violence). This will also require a reprimand, but the teacher should understand the provocation occasioned by racist taunts, and in any case, they should not overlook, and should be seen not to overlook, the original abuse.
- The school should have a policy and procedures, known to everyone, for dealing with racial abuse, name-calling and other forms of bullying.

Application

Educating and gender

Sexism, by which I mean prejudice and discrimination based on gender, which relegates women to a subservient and inferior status, is prevalent in this and other societies. It cuts across other forms of inequality in that women and men are also in those other categorizations. Thus, working-class women may experience discrimination in different ways from middle-class women but in both cases the women are in an unequal power relation with working- and middle-class men. The same is true across ethnic groups too. Sexism, being an unequal power relation between women and men, also cuts into every area of our lives, entering into our homes and families as well as into our workplaces and schools.

Sexism is harmful to girls and women in promoting restrictive and inaccurate stereotypes (nice girls don't argue) and to a lesser extent boys and men are also harmed by stereotypes of masculinity (brave boys don't cry). Additionally, such is the scale of sexual discrimination, women end up with less interesting and well-paid work and less powerful and prestigious positions and far more of the chores. In education, for example, although two-thirds of the primary school teachers are women, more heads are men. In secondary schools, although nearly half the teachers are women, most heads are men. In schools, do the girls do most of the clearing up?

Research has borne out what many parents and teachers were already aware off. Boys hog the limelight and demand more attention than girls. They dominate classroom discussion and are more noisy and less cooperative. These differences result in differential teacher behaviour. Boys receive more teacher attention and time. Teachers ask them more questions, give them more individual attention and more praise. Teachers also tend to have higher academic expectations of the boys. It is not surprising, then, that boys tend to become more confident and assertive than the girls.

Advice

- Subject choices

  In school, time-tabling must allow for girls and boys to make sensible subject choices with full counselling and information on how early decisions condition later options. If girls opt out of maths as an examination subject, for example, do they understand what limits this may impose in terms of future training and study?

- The curriculum

  The curriculum for both girls and boys should counter sexism. As we saw in the case of racism, this involves a permeation of the curricular in terms of eradicating biased language and assumptions and avoiding stereotyping books and other learning resources. It involves re-orientating biases in the subjects of the curriculum themselves. For example:

  - Is History presented as the study of great men?
  - Are the Literature texts, especially in poetry and drama, all by male authors?
  - Is there some direct teaching about sexism, too? This is a subject about which the pupils can readily draw on their own experiences, since we treat girls and boys very differently, from babyhood onwards.

- Single sex schools and groups

  As adolescence approaches, girls may fear that to be clever will lead to peer rejection, especially by boys. In response to these facts, some mixed schools have established single sex groups for subjects such as maths.

Family background

Social class is both one of the categories within inequality and a dimension to most of the rest. Black people and people with disabilities tend to be disproportionately in the lower economic classes. This is not surprising as they face the employment and education discrimination associated with race and disability. Women, despite the equal pay legislation, as a group earn far less than men.

In education we need to be aware on the inter-relatedness and complexity of inequality. For example, a study by Peter Foster ((1990), *Policy and Practice in Multicultural and Antiracist Education* (London: Routledge) revealed that in a particular multi-ethnic secondary school the white as well as the black children were badly failed. The inequality between schools produces lower achieving schools – the teachers' expectations of all pupils is low and emphasis is on control rather than on academic achievement.

Schools are largely middle-class institutions in terms of their ethos, assumptions, values and teaching force. Books reflect middle-class norms and lifestyles. Regional dialects and accents are less valued and standard English is the rewarded goal.

We all make biased judgements. For example, people are known to be influenced by accent in their evaluation of the intelligence of what is actually being said. Similarly, in a mixed catchment area studies have shown that even where teachers genuinely intend to stream children into ability groups they are influenced by home background. Children from middle-class homes tended to be allocated to the upper streams and those from the manual working class to the lower streams. Moreover, dirty or badly clothed children and those from large families tend to be placed in the lower streams, regardless of ability. The streaming then influences future performance.

It is important to remember that there are many different kinds of families: one parent, two gay parents, an extended family, grandmother or other relative as carer, foster family, families with a step-parent, etc. Indeed, the traditional two-parent family is becoming much less of a norm.

Advice

Key points

- It is important that teachers have high expectations of all their pupils and provide good careers advice and do not limit the horizon of any child.

- Teachers must recognize all families as families – both in practical terms and in attitudes conveyed.

- Teachers and governors who share the background of and live in the same area as most of the school's clientele will have much to contribute from their daily experiences.

  - For example, it is the teacher or a governor who lives in a local council house who is most likely to draw attention to the lack, for many pupils, of a quiet study area or a centrally heated unshared bedroom. The school then might provide evening homework study facilities to the benefit of its working-class pupils.

- The ethos of the school is crucial. Teachers and governors have an important role to play in helping to create the kind of school where every child is valued.

- Just as a non-authoritarian approach to childrearing correlates with lower levels of prejudice within the developing child, so a non-authoritarian, child-centred school will discourage bullying, and by developing security and self-esteem encourage each pupil, whatever their social background, to realize their learning potential. In such a school:

  - teachers make encouraging rather than sarcastic remarks;

  - praise rather then punish;

  - stimulate rather than bore;

  - are open to parents and to new ideas.

- Teachers and governors, indeed all members of the school community, must help to create warm, innovative, democratic, empowering institutions, whether located in drab housing estates, decaying inner cities or leafy suburbs. Thus education might begin to reduce rather than perpetuate inequalities between, as well as within, all our schools.

Application

Why is inclusion important?

The damage from exclusion

A school fails if it fails to make children want to be there and to enjoy learning. A child who does not feel at ease in school, who does not feel valued and accepted, will not fulfil their educational potential.

If home and school seem incompatible and completely separate the child is less likely to accept the learning and values offered by the school. Indeed, a school that leaves the child feeling excluded (alienated by the curriculum or rejected by staff or peer group) has his or her self-esteem damaged by the experience and will be an unhappy child.

At an even more serious level, schools may fail to prevent bullying. Bullied children may lose all their self-confidence and become cowed. Such children are frightened and unhappy, in the most extreme cases, to the point of committing suicide.

The experience of exclusion can arise from:

- an alien curriculum and resources
- teacher/staff hostility
- peer-group rejection and bullying
- unfair treatment through the school structure, staff or pupils.

Exclusion results in a range of negative effects, including:

- less effective learning
- damage to self-esteem
- unhappiness and apprehension at school
- extremes of fear and depression.

Advice

Inclusion is important because exclusive practice damages children and their learning while inclusive practice removes unfair barriers and promotes respect

Children as a group are perhaps the most vulnerable group of all. In order to protect all children regardless of their social group, and to provide justice and care there have been attempts to base policy and practice on the notion of the rights of the child. For example, the 1959 United Nations Declaration on the Rights of the Child produced a list of children's rights and this notion of rights has perhaps informed more recent legislation in Britain, such as the Children's Act.

The 1959 United Nations Declaration on the Rights of the Child stated that every child has the right to:

- affection, love and understanding
- adequate nutrition and medical care
- special care if handicapped
- full opportunity for play or recreation
- be the first to receive relief in times of disaster
- a name and nationality
- education about how to be a useful member of society
- be brought up in the spirit of peace and universal brotherhood
- enjoy these rights regardless of race, sex, religion, national or social origin.

Application

Inclusive learning and values

The National Curriculum requires the development of personal, social, moral, emotional, cultural and spiritual values. Values, just as any part of the National Curriculum, are learned. Thus, the National Curriculum recognizes that as well as the distinctively educational values of rationality and criticality, there are various other kinds of educationally relevant values too. We must not simply educate minds, attending to only a child's cognitive development, we must educate character, emotion, imagination and spirit. Education is of the whole child and this holistic conception of educational development is in keeping with developing values as an integral part of the whole curriculum. To learn the values implicit in inclusion is thus a contribution to the children's values education.

All of the values required by the National Curriculum have an inclusive dimension.

Thus personal values such as personal responsibility, independence, self-confidence and self-esteem are just those values that will help children to counter the bully and bullying.

Social values such as cooperation, sharing and friendship will mean that children are much more likely to be inclusive and kind in their dealings across social groups.

Emotional qualities and values of empathy, creativity and love will also mean that children care about each other.

Moral principals and values embracing both justice and care will tend to encourage a sense of fairness as well as the caring attributes.

Spiritual values such as wonder at the natural world, and respect for world religions will also contribute to an acceptance of diversity.

One could sum this up by pointing out that inclusive practices and inclusive values are inescapably part of good education. An unhappy child does not learn effectively. To ensure that each child has the well-being that comes from feeling included is thus an educational goal. There is solid educational value in inclusion.

National Curriculum cross-curricula values

The values dimension includes personal, social, moral, emotional, spiritual and multicultural values.

Examples of personal values: self-confidence, independence, responsibility, self-esteem.

Examples of social values: friendship, sharing, sympathy, cooperation.

Examples of moral values: justice/fairness, care/compassion, honesty.

Examples of emotional values: creativity, empathy, love, kindness.

Examples of spiritual values: awe/wonder, appreciation of the natural world, respect for world faiths.

Examples of multicultural values: inclusion of minority ethnic group children and cultures.

Obviously these value domains overlap. For example, kindness is a social and a moral value.

Inclusion

A good 'values' curriculum will be fair and humane to children of all backgrounds, tending against prejudice, discrimination and bullying. 'Inclusion' will have regard to disabled children.

Family background

A good 'values' curriculum will also be sensitive and respectful to diversity of other kinds too (examples: a child's appearance, family structures and differences).

Our schools

Therefore, inclusive schools will reflect these values and include cultural pluralism and children with special needs. Such schools will *not* perpetuate stereotypes or biased assumptions about 'differences' of these various kinds.

Application

Justice and care

Another way of considering the values built into inclusion is to consider the requirements of moral education, central to which has been an emphasis on justice. Kohlberg's hugely influential work, for example, conceived moral education in terms of developing children's ability to reason about moral dilemmas involving the acquiring of understanding about moral principals such as justice. Feminist philosophers such as Carol Gilligan argued that an undervalued element in this approach is the recognition of the moral importance of care and compassion.

Thus the two most significant values of morality could be said to be justice and care – the very values at the heart of inclusion.

Justice: it is because we see it is right to treat children equally well and wrong to discriminate to some children's disadvantage that inclusion is partly about the promotion of equal educational opportunity and justice.

Care: in addition to wanting to be fair, it is because of our empathy and compassion that we want all children to flourish and want no child to feel alienated or unhappy at school or to be bullied there.

It is the same moral values and qualities (justice and care) that we seek to pass onto the children, by example and through direct teaching, as significant elements in their own moral education and development.

Work on moral education encouraged the notion of a 'just community' school, and some schools have attempted to develop a just community school in which parents and children are involved in the decision making and where governors and teachers show by example how to relate to other people in humane and non-hierarchical ways. This approach takes seriously the idea that children learn from the hidden as well as from the overt curriculum, from example and from participation. The process by which children learn is important, indeed is part of what they learn. This learning from school processes and relationships informs their political and moral understanding. Education is not just about more directly utilitarian knowledge and skills.

Advice

Empathy

- Use stories to help the children to develop empathy. By identifying with a character they like in a story they enjoy, children are learning to understand other people's viewpoints and feelings.

- Let children write their own stories involving a hero or heroine that undergoes experiences that make the character unhappy. This, too, helps the children to enter into another's feelings with empathy and to gain an understanding of human motivation.

- Look for books with a sympathetic central character who experiences unfair and unfeeling treatment, such as, at primary level, *The Silver Sword* by Ian Serrailler (Red Fox, 2003) or at secondary level, *Private Peaceful* by Michael Morpurgo (HarperCollins, 2004).

- My own books with Routledge seek to develop inclusive values in the early years and at the Key Stages 1 and 2. They provide stories and learning activities to this end. They include:

  Early Years Stories for the Foundation Stage (2006)

  Stories for Assembly and the Classroom (2003)

  Stories for Inclusive Schools (2003)

  Stories for Circle Time and Assembly (2005).

Justice

- Outline some moral dilemmas to the children and have group discussions about what one ought to do – giving recognition to points that the children make which rely on recognition of universal moral principals of justice and fairness.

Making changes, removing barriers and promoting respect

We have seen that inclusion has both a structural and an educational component. The structural component relates to dismantling any established routines that have been discriminating against children from various disadvantaged groups. The educational component relates to providing a curriculum, resources and ethos that counter social prejudice and promote respect for other people and other groups.

No school is perfect – perfection being a utopian ideal. Though institutional and attitudinal changes are not easy to achieve, all schools can make changes towards inclusion.

Change often requires patience, tact, determination and strategy! The educational system is diverse. Power and authority is distributed between various groups and individuals, including central and local government, governors, headteachers and teachers, parents and pupils. Change will therefore be complex, slow and piecemeal – operating at various interacting levels. Frameworks provided by central government and the LEA constrain but do not determine what schools will be like. Individual schools have considerable, but not complete freedom within these imposed structures and constraints, and what goes on in each school's various classrooms will be considerably influenced by its individual teachers. Inclusive progress will therefore require changes at three levels; that of the individual teacher, the individual institution and at central/local government level. All three levels interact and are influenced by many pressures.

An individual teacher is most likely to influence his or her school by working collectively with other like-minded individuals in pressure groups of various kinds. The process of change is important and the more people that are involved in that process the more effective the changes are likely to be. Moreover, such democratically wide involvement is consonant with inclusive values.

- At the outset we took note of helpful resources that a school may already have in place. Consider how these can be strengthened and built on.

- The training of all staff and governors in inclusive issues is extremely important. All have their part to play. Consider devoting a staff training day to inclusion.

- Consider setting up (or proposing the setting up) of a working party on any relevant aspect of inclusion. For example, a working party to:

  - Draw up a school equal opportunity policy. This should state the school equal opportunity policy with clear objectives, designated responsibilities, implementation advice and monitoring procedures.

  - Draw up an anti-bullying policy. This should contain similar sections to those suggested for the equal opportunity policy above.

  - Analyse existing school resources for diversity and to make recommendations for improvements.

  - Set up relevant working parties to produce guidelines for an inclusive system of pastoral care.

It is not suggested that all these groups operate simultaneously!

- Working groups should seek to be representative and democratic. To be representative they would, for example, include: a senior staff member such as the head or deputy; two teaching staff members; two auxiliary staff members; a governor; a parent and two school pupils. Each of these representatives should, where possible, be elected by their relevant group – staff, governors, parents, pupils and should, for accountability, report back to their group

- If there is an individual in a partner school or college or in the local university or local community who has relevant experience and knowledge, perhaps they could be invited to join the committee/working group.

- Such working groups not only create a useful set of guidelines or policy statement, the process of doing so is itself an *educative* one for all concerned.

Application

The *how* of inclusion: Curriculum and resources

Curriculum development and inclusion

Inclusion should permeate the curriculum. All parts of the curriculum should have a multicultural dimension, include and cater for people with a variety of impairments and suit both boys and girls. All areas of the curriculum should avoid stereotypes and encourage inclusive values. By 'all parts of the curriculum' is meant all the six foundation areas in the early years; the National Curriculum and project work covering the National Curriculum in the primary school; and all the subject areas such as English, Science and Geography, etc., and the cross-curricular themes in secondary schools.

Essentially permeation is not about bolting bits onto the curriculum but a pervasive interweaving of an inclusive perspective. Such permeation often begins with small-scale projects undertaken by the classroom teacher, moving onto the development of initiatives across the school and incorporating evaluation of the school policy and ethos that has emerged.

Such permeation contrasts with tokenism. It involves all aspects and parts of the curriculum and not just sample bits of content here and there. We have also noted the importance of shared democratic values within the inclusive perspective – together with opportunities for pupils to understand a variety of ways of life and forms of thought.

Direct teaching about prejudice and discrimination should also be provided.

Advice

How can inclusion be achieved through curriculum development and permeate learning resources? We need curriculum development and good resources in the foundational early years, at Key Stages 1, 2, 3 and 4 and for post-school education

Key points

- An inclusive curriculum is not just about adding minority elements such as cuisine, art forms, etc. It is about recognizing the validity of more than one way of doing things. This involves a reorientation of viewpoint.

- It is about recognizing that all human beings share the same basic needs and emotions.

- Where minority cuisine, arts, etc., are explored, teachers can learn from minority ethnic group parents and children. Learning becomes a cooperative process rather than a top-down clump of information.

- Themes, topics and projects are immeasurably richer when they move away from ethnocentricity to genuine diversity and inclusion.

- Progressive and positive schools will give support to teachers and pupils who are involved in inclusive curriculum development.

Some of the ways that permeation can be achieved are:

- to be sensitive to language used, and assumptions made;
- to be sensitive to the hidden as well as to the overt curriculum;
- to use examples, (names, celebrations, etc.) which draw on minority group experience and minority group cultures;
- to remember the inventors, thinkers, writers and other 'great' women and men (especially women who are often overlooked) from minority ethnic groups and including distinguished disabled people;
- to recognise the contribution of 'other' cultures, traditions, civilisations and countries to human knowledge and achievement.

Application

Inclusion in the curriculum

Teachers need to pay attention to the hidden curriculum, to the unexamined judgements about what is the norm or what constitutes acceptable dress, speech and so on, so that a genuine and unforced pluralism begins to permeate the whole of a child's school experience. Inclusion incorporates approach attitudes, learning materials and implicit assumptions. In addition, a pluralist and multicultural dimension can be developed within all the specific subjects that make up the National Curriculum. A child's education should include some experience of the major cultural traditions that make up our society and provide opportunities to learn from them. Children from cultural minority groups need to see that their own languages, religions, lifestyles and histories are recognized and valued by the school.

With primary school project work, a multicultural approach can also be adopted. One can look at how common needs and purposes lie behind the diversity of ways of life. Principles of nutrition, for example, can be taught using dishes and diet patterns from a variety of cultural traditions, and aesthetic appreciation can be developed by reference to a variety of cultural art forms, for example, Caribbean poetry as well as the English romantics.

Where schools implement a common curriculum at each age level, this should be modified to meet the differing needs of children of differing abilities. Where schools run different curriculum options for different children, they should be presented as being appropriate to different children's interests but not as hierarchies in which some are intrinsically superior to others. And within each class, the teacher should use a range of strategies to take account of differing abilities – for example, allowing children to complete the same work at different rates, allowing some children to complete work in simplified form, and from time to time setting different group or individual work for different children.

Organization

- Mixed ability groups are inclusive.
- Teachers should employ a wide range of learning strategies. Group work is likely to be particularly fruitful. Groups could sometimes devise their own learning agendas.
- Teachers should see themselves as facilitators, allowing pupils space to work out their own ideas and follow their interests.
- An integrated humanities approach has more potential than separate subjects in the primary school. It encourages teachers to work together across their own interests and specialisms.
- Teachers could have agreed checklists for selecting inclusive materials and reviewing current practice.

Perspective

- All courses should have an international perspective.
- All courses should emphasize links and interdependence between social groups.
- All courses should give due consideration to the historical background of contemporary issues.
- All courses should develop pupils' critical skills.
- Humanities courses have particular responsibility for dealing with value-laden issues.
- Schools should seek a 'black perspective' on the overall coverage of their multicultural curriculum.
- Courses should emphasize common features of human societies.

Content

1. All courses should include an inclusive perspective within the curriculum content, where possible using authentic voices.
2. Discrimination should be dealt with in an explicit way at clearly identifiable points throughout the curriculum.
3. The humanities have a particular responsibility for giving black and disabled pupils and all pupils the opportunity to talk about their experiences of discrimination.

Application

Bias in learning resources

It has been rightly said that a teacher with understanding of inclusion and poor resources is immeasurably better than a teacher with excellent resources and no understanding. After all, to enable children to critique poor resources can be excellent educative learning in critical thinking, in media studies, in social awareness and understanding, in literacy skills, etc. Nevertheless, good resources are useful to time-pressed teachers and good, inclusive resources do exist.

The starting point is to be aware of existing school resources. Identify the positive and avoid the negative except for critique purposes!

Since the movement to multicultural education some decades ago the resources that incorporate a variety of cultural traditions and children from all ethnic groups have greatly increased and much of this material is very good indeed. However, there is a lack of stories where the hero or heroine is a disabled child. It is surely important that all children see disabled child heroes and heroines actively solving problems in a whole variety of contexts and situations. Disabled children need and deserve to see that disabled characters are included in the world of books. They will enjoy reading more if they can read about children who share their impairment. It is equally important that non-disabled children read stories with disabled characters. Their omission carries an implicit message that they are less interesting and less valued. Such messages affect the children's developing attitudes and beliefs.

Some children are from both disabled and from minority ethnic groups. These children should also see their counterparts in the books they read. Such children face two exclusion frontiers as it were.

Bias in resources can occur from both omission and commission. The omission or absence of minority ethnic group or disabled children in stories, or girls in science books, or minority cultures in art, music or literature is an anti-inclusion omission. In addition some books are explicitly racist, sexist, disablist or homophobic and not suitable to show children. Bias of both kinds can occur in the text (the language used), in the content material and in the illustrations.

Advice

Checklist for bias through omission:

- Are some of the books written from the standpoint of the multicultural society?
- Do they show 'other' religions, languages, lifestyles as valuable?
- Do the books include disabled people as valued citizens?
- Is the experience of disabled people part of the resources?
- Do the resources show equal regard for and acceptance of different ethnic groups?
- Are there strong female characters as role models for girls?
- Are there black, brown, disabled and female characters shown in positions of authority and responsibility and so on.
- Are cultural minorities, disabled people and other minority groups present in both the text and the illustrations? Are they presented in a matter of fact, accepting, positive way?

Checklist for bias through commission:

- Is there evidence of tokenism or stereotyping in the text?
- Does the language convey prejudice by use of pejorative words such as uncivilized, backward, crippled, or use linguistic stereotyping. For example, white equals pure, black equals evil?
- Do the illustrations show evidence of caricature or stereotyping?
- Are 'other' cultures judged against a European norm? Are non-European cultures seen exclusively in terms of the exotic? Is the superiority of European cultures assumed and is it seen as the desirable norm for all people?
- Are historical events seen exclusively from a European viewpoint? Do non-European countries appear to have no history until 'discovered' by Europeans?
- Is poverty attributed to lack of western technology and expertise? In short, is there no good Development Education?
- Does the book reinforce the image of a power structure in which white, able-bodied men make all the decisions?
- Does the book contain anything that is damaging to the self-esteem or to the developing attitudes of the children in your class?

Application

Positive learning resources

'Resources' is a term that embraces a very wide range. It includes local organizations, teacher-made materials, fiction and non-fiction books, development education materials, cultural artefacts, bibliographies of multicultural books and/or periodicals, book shops, films, videos, DVDs, slides, music, etc. Early learning resources also include picture books, dolls, puppets, jigsaws, card games – all of which can include images of black and brown children and, where obtainable, children with impairments, for example, a wheelchair user. With a good stock of such resources teachers can draw on these to build up and enrich inclusive teaching, keeping inclusive criteria in mind.

Children are affected by the images presented to them. Images are powerful attitude formers, as parents and teachers know. Most children like to conform to the 'norm' and tend to disapprove of deviants from it. In order to prevent their pupils' acquisition of false beliefs and prejudiced attitudes, it is part of the teachers' duty to look critically at the books and other learning materials which she or he plans to use. One can then make a professional judgement about which to use and which to discard.

Of course resources for buying positive materials are limited. Teachers can explore the possibility of borrowing books and other resources from libraries and LEA centres and services, and when making their own learning resources can very much keep inclusive criteria in mind.

Most books found in schools are written by white, able-bodied, middle-class authors and reflect white middle-class values and lifestyles. The movement to multicultural education produced much good material written by black authors. There are several bibliographies that suggest criteria for the assessment of bias and which provide details about quality inclusive books

Listed below are examples of different kinds of resources:

Organizations: Local

- Local multicultural education centres
- Libraries
- Museums
- African and Asian resource centres, music and folk songs
- LEA support services
- Local arts associations
- Local Asian shops for cooking utensils and ingredients.

Organisations: National

- DfES
- Voluntary organizations such as Oxfam (Education Department).

Developing your own resources

Teachers who are working on projects and resources of a wider relevance, useful to more than one school, might be eligible for funding. Look at:

- The Directory of Grant Making Trusts
- Minority newspapers
- Specialist shops.

Books/Bibliographies

There are vast numbers of books and helpful bibliographies which can be 'googled' or accessed via Amazon or in the children's sections of a good library. For example:

- *Diversity in Children's Lives: Children's Books and Classroom Helps* (2002), ed. Molly Westin, lists books that feature positive images of children and adults who are culturally, linguistically and ability-diverse. Each entry includes title, author, diversity type and a brief explanation of content. This resource is available on the internet at www.fpg.unc.edu/~pfi/pdfs/diversitybooklist.pdf

Application

Early years: Inclusive learning in the six domains

The early years are educationally crucial. Here the foundations are laid for lifelong learning. Here, children who have not yet acquired critical skills absorb the values (the good and the prejudicial) found in their world. It is, therefore, important that the pre-school child benefits from enjoyable learning and peer interaction, structured to take account of the early learning goals of the six early year domains. These domains should all benefit from an inclusive dimension. In this way the children will receive a sound preparation for 'proper' school.

Personal social and emotional development is particularly important for values education. We know that even very young children acquire the social prejudices of their society (see Milner, D. (1983) *Children and Race: Ten Years On* (London: Ward Lock) and we must seek to ensure that positive inclusive experiences and resources are part of their world. The developing self needs to grow self-confidence, and in relation with others needs to learn the inclusive moral attributes of sharing and empathy, and to learn to be interested in different people and different ways of life, rather than to be fearful or disapproving.

Young children will absorb parental and teacher attitudes. All childcare students need to learn something about the relative and often multiple disadvantages faced by some children in the inner-city areas and to understand about racial discrimination and about the development of prejudices in the formative years. They should learn about different ways of life, different child-rearing practices and different family structures. It is important that childcare staff involve parents and carers and build good relationships with them.

There may be implications here for awareness training for childcare students and practitioners and for more recruitment of childcare students from the minority ethnic groups, including some who are bilingual in the minority languages. Similarly, a childcare member of staff who has an impairment will be a role model for children with special needs.

Advice

The six early learning domains are:

- Personal, social and emotional development

  For an example of an inclusive learning activity use: *The Adventures of the Little Tin Tortoise*, a self-esteem story with activities for teachers, parents and carers by Deborah Plummer, published by Jessica Kingsley (2005).

- Communication, language and literacy

  Go around the circle and ask the children to say whether each of these words is a kind word or a mean word: share, smile, quarrel, gentle, slap, selfish, helping, bullying, ignoring, playing. If the answer is not what you expect, ask why the child thinks that (they may have a good reason, for example, the slap of waves on your feet feels kind). Go round the circle and ask the children for more kind and mean words.

- Mathematical development

  Give the children pictures with positive inclusive images. They then cut the card or picture into a four-piece jigsaw, and then fit their picture together. You can then ask them to swap and fit another child's picture together. This develops mathematical understanding through the understanding of shapes and forms.

- Knowledge and understanding of the world

  Collect a range of pictures of people (including black people, disabled people and women), all of whom are doing helpful jobs. Have the children identify who helps us in the picture, for example, nurse, fire person, lollipop person, teacher, etc.

- Physical development

  Focus on healthy eating using examples from a range of cultural groups when you illustrate the food groups.

- Creative development

  Role play in pairs: the children could role play some of the kind and mean words, a sharing action, smiling and making friends, quarrelling and making up, bullying and what to do about it … etc.

Inclusive learning at Key Stages 1 and 2: 7–11

A holistic approach to learning occurs much more in primary education than in secondary. Provided primary school teachers recognize the implicit values in what is taught and how it is taught they will be in a good position to ensure that inclusive values become an integral part of the children's classroom activities. Inclusive values include: self-confidence, co-operation, sharing, friendship with another 'different' from me, empathy, care, fairness, respect for 'other' ways of life and for world religions.

In more explicit mode, inclusive education at Key Stages 1 and 2 will include: learning about prejudice, exploring difference, dealing with bullying.

For 'different' children to be *successfully* included (or integrated) we need teacher awareness about bullying and who is likely to be bullied and how to develop positive attitudes and values towards diversity. Mainstream children need to develop understanding and acceptance of the 'different' child and to acquire a positive self-image and self-respect.

During Key Stages 1 and 2 the children's horizons widen considerably. One could conceive this as a widening circle of values starting with the self and widening out to others, then to the world, and then to the world of values themselves. Each ring offers an opportunity to develop inclusive learning activities to promote:

- self-confidence (ring 1)
- empathy and social skills (ring 2)
- awareness of other places and ways of life (ring 3)
- an understanding of values (ring 4).

The use of story, with its inherent emphasis on values and emotions, is a great tool for the development of empathy and the development of literacy. Chosen wisely, the literature you read with the children is crucial for inclusive education.

Advice

- Inclusive values can be developed during circle time and discussion time, and can be implicit in literacy goals. For example:

  Self-esteem is part of listening and speaking with confidence.

  Empathy is involved in understanding characters in stories.

  Co-operation is involved in group work.

- Examples of learning activities for each of the rings of values:

  Self-confidence (ring 1)

  In a circle ask the children one good thing about themselves (for example: 'I help my mum', 'I was brave at the dentist') and one good thing about another person (for example: 'Anne is good at writing'). The teacher could then say a good thing about each child. In pairs the children could also find out good things about themselves and about their partner.

  Empathy (ring 2)

  In pairs the children could write a short play in which one character has a problem involving some sadness and the other character shows that they understand and helps in some way.

  Awareness of difference (ring 3)

  Let the children draw around their hands and select paint to reproduce their skin tone. Explore the differences between the finished painted hands: size, shape, colour. Lead into a discussion about how we are all unique (otherwise people would be boring!) and yet we all have so much in common, too.

  Understanding values (ring 4)

  Make a class values circle, chart or frieze. First explain the difference between valuing something and liking something (i.e. value has merit for everyone, liking is a preference for the individual. Examples of values: honesty, kindness, a beautiful picture, a rainbow, a good book. Examples of preferences: chocolate, football, or a particular book). Each child could write one value on a card, perhaps create a colourful border around the edge of the card. These could then be stuck on a poster, or along a long class frieze.

Application

Inclusive learning at Key Stages 3 and 4: 11–14

In secondary schools children have a subject-based curriculum, and, as has been previously discussed, inclusive curriculum material and inclusive values should permeate this curriculum. Inclusion has implications for all the subjects of the National Curriculum, and for the cross-curricular areas, too. As teachers in all the subject areas need to develop their subject to encompass inclusive material, they can discover helpful guidelines and resources through browsing the catalogues of publishers and making contact with relevant national and local organizations, as well as by taking advantage of relevant INSET (In Service Education of Teachers).

In addition, secondary teachers prepare pupils for their subject-based GCSE examinations and for entering further or higher education or the world of work. Research has consistently indicated that some minority ethnic group children and disabled children do less well in their examinations. Teachers need to demand high standards and have high expectations of children – expectations that match the child's capacities, not their social group.

An inclusive education should contribute to, not hinder, the attainment of intellectual knowledge and skills and examination achievements. Multicultural education, for example, is not an alternative to such success but should be consonant with it. Some groups of children are underachieving in terms of qualifications gained by the end of their secondary schooling, including boys from the poorer social classes, and this points to a failure of secondary education that must change in order to address this underachievement.

All children deserve as part of their secondary education an equal chance to learn more about vocational training and educational opportunities and about careers and career paths beyond schools. Informed choices can only be made by informed children and parents. Good careers education is an important part of inclusive education in the secondary years.

Advice

Resources

- There are several kinds of relevant books for secondary school teachers to seek out. These include good fiction with sympathetic minority characters and good subject-based inclusive non-fiction.

- When browsing the catalogues of reputable publishers look out for inclusive materials.

- Many educational publishers now have regard to multicultural education. Look out for minority ethnic group authors as part of this.

- Jessica Kingsley Publishers is particularly good in relation to inclusive education and disability, including specialism in autism for example. Catalogues available from: Jessica Kingsley Publishers, 116 Pentonville Road, London N1 9JB, UK.

- There are many good books available on CD. Choose those with an implicit inclusion dimension and the children will simultaneously develop listening skills, concentration and love of stories – increasing their likely enjoyment of print books too.

- English teachers should review their book boxes against inclusive criteria.

Examples of Inclusion in Secondary Education

Some examples of inclusion in the secondary curriculum include: in literature good writers in English of various cultural and racial backgrounds; in drama the children could explore their own experiences and dilemmas; in social studies the teacher can begin to examine with the children the topic of race relations in Britain or of sexism or of the disability rights movement; in home economics teachers can incorporate the traditional dishes of a variety of cultural groups; even in maths and science an awareness of the possibility of alternative logics and alternative scientific paradigms, of the viable alternatives to a society based on technology and of the contributions of black peoples and of women and of disabled individuals can be incorporated. Here, as elsewhere, inclusive learning aids and examples can be used. One important curriculum component that has led the way in such developments for many schools is religious education. Many teachers have introduced a multifaith dimension into their religious education promoting respect for the variety of world faiths.

Application

Beyond school: Inclusive education 15+

Academic education

Children who stay on at school to do A level study, and university students, also have a subject-based curriculum. These subjects ought to be permeated with inclusive material and values. At these higher levels, pupils' critical thinking skills are more advanced, too, and being further developed. Thus, their ability to detect bias and prejudiced perspectives can be both practised and sharpened.

Further education

Further/adult education colleges provide vocational training and recreational activities. Colleges need to consult with community organizations about special needs within communities.

However, the setting up of appropriate courses is not by itself sufficient. Reception and admissions policy should seek to make students feel welcome and college counselling services need to take account of the special problems faced by ethnic minority students and disabled students: job discrimination, language, grants, police harassment, nationality citizenship status, stereotyping, etc. Use of minority languages in notices and other literature, catering and cultural events should all reflect the college clientele.

Ideally two full-time senior members of staff should have special responsibility for inclusion, developing structures that work for minority students: ethnic minority students and disabled students respectively. These staff members should consider the promotion of access courses, alternative routes into acquiring vocational and/or academic qualifications, giving consideration to financial support for disadvantaged students. For female students the importance of college crèche facilities cannot be overstated.

Advice

- College courses

  College courses should, of course, also be permeated by inclusive issues and values, using positive books and other resources. Students should be educated for life and work in a diverse society. In addition, inclusive awareness courses should be provided. These would have regard to racism, sexism, disability awareness and awareness about homophobia. In such work, experiential approaches are more productive than lecturing!

- Experiential resources

  These are simulation/role playing games produced by voluntary organizations and some publishers. For example BaFa BaFa. This provides material for a simulation game which aims to demonstrate the difficulties and problems of two cultures coming face to face with each other.

- Further reading – Further education

  BaFa BaFa, pp. 82–5 in Hicks, D. (1981), *Minorities* (London and Oxford: Heinemann).

  Hyland, T., 'Learning, Work, Community', in Field, J. and Leicester, M. (2000) *Lifelong Learning: Education Across the Lifespan* (London: Routledge).

- Further reading – Higher education

  Leicester, M. (1993), *Race for a Change in Continuing and Higher Education* (Buckingham: Open University Press).

  Cotterill, P. *et al.* (eds) (2007), *Challenges and Negotiations for Women in Higher Education* (Dordrecht: Springer).

- Further reading – Lifelong learning

  Field, J. and Leicester, M. (2000), *Lifelong Learning: Education Across the Lifespan* (London: Routledge).

  DFEE (1998), 'The Learning Age: A Renaissance for a New Britain', www.lifelonglearning.dfee.gov.uk/greenpaper/index.htm

Application

The *how* of inclusion: Inclusion in the classroom

An inclusive pedagogy

1   Learning styles and variety of learning activities

Pupils and adults have different learning styles. Some of us learn best when presented with abstract ideas that stimulate our interest – the concrete examples coming after. More of us, and most young children, need to have the learning material rooted in our own experience, with the concrete and particular assimilated first and the universal implications and abstract principles emerging later. Some of us like to listen or read, some of us prefer to undertake learning tasks and others to engage in structured discussion, etc. A variety of teaching approaches will ensure that different learning styles are catered for. Moreover, a variety of pedagogical approaches tends to keep the learner more interested across the day or week. In other words, teachers should structure a day (primary) or a teaching session (secondary) so that there is some variety in the learning activities included. In addition since we often don't assimilate new material after just one exposure, a variety of approaches to the same material gives us the required familiarity for long-term learning to be achieved.

2   Pedagogical techniques

Inclusion means that children with special needs should be, where possible, integrated into ordinary classes. There are huge training implications here in terms of gaining appropriate techniques for different learning impairments – sensory or of learning ability, for example. Good practice tends to benefit all the learners.

Advice

It is important to develop inclusive practice in the classroom at all stages of education; the early years, primary, secondary and post school.

- Vary both the organization and the type of the learning task.
    - Organizational/structural variety:

        group work – have differentiated tasks toward a common good

        work in pairs

        circle time discussion

        class outings

        link schemes – work well (see Lewis, A. (1995) *Children's Understanding of Disability.* (London: Routledge))
    - Learning tasks for the children can include:

        reading (aloud or to oneself) writing, listening, speaking

        project work

        painting

        problem solving.

- Seek out training in meeting special needs in the classroom – including INSET provision and discussion with colleagues.

- There is, of course, a difference between learning difficulty and difference. A child with *learning difficulties* has an impairment of their ability to learn in some area. This impairment tends to be specific. For example, don't assume that a child with impairment of their ability with number concepts will necessarily have poor language skills. A child who has a *learning difference* may be a bright child (for example, some autistic children) but he or she tends to view the world differently and thus to learn differently to the majority.

Application

Classroom ethos

By classroom ethos is meant the 'culture' or 'atmosphere' of a particular classroom. It includes the relationships between teacher and pupils, and pupil and pupil, the 'look' or visual environment and the kind of routines and behaviours established. Let us assume that a teacher has received awareness training and also has developed an inclusive curriculum and uses inclusive resources. How can she or he ensure that this more nebulous *general atmosphere* is as inclusive and enabling as possible?

Certainly the teacher will treat all the pupils fairly and empathetically, not showing favouritism and thus setting a good example to the children. She or he will also expect good behaviour and pupil engagement with the learning tasks.

The children's work will be on display, with pleasing and pluralist posters and pictures. There will be natural objects (for example, plants or a nature table) and interesting and beautiful cultural artefacts, objects and fabrics. This visual environment should reflect our multicultural society and the educational projects with which the children are currently engaged.

Some of the visual images should counter stereotypes. (For example, in relation to a *people who care for us* project, a photograph of a black female fire person, or a white male nurse, or a consultant in a wheelchair).

Particularly in multicultural schools, languages other than English should be included in the notices and displays.

In the primary school the teacher is the key to the pastoral care of the children. In the secondary school, children move from a small, or relatively small primary school, to a larger secondary comprehensive, with thet additional pressure of adolescence. Good secondary schools, therefore, recognize the need for a system of pastoral care as a key component in the organization and management of the institution.

- The person-centred teacher will:
  - Understand their pupil's experiences.
  - Show respect for every pupil.
  - Build a genuine relationship with each pupil.
  - Build the self-confidence of pupils.
  - Be open with pupils.
  - Give praise and encouragement.
  - Be responsive to pupil ideas.
  - Engage in formal didactic teaching less often.
- In secondary schools, student-centred teachers will:
  - Extend the range of role models with whom ethnic minority and disabled students can identify.
  - Prepare vulnerable (out-group) pupils for dealing with the discrimination they will meet in the world of work.
  - Provide useful skills and knowledge relating to the labour market.
- A positive classroom ethos embraces:
  - a pluralist curriculum
  - a differentiated curriculum
  - resources
  - visual environment
  - religious differences (dress etc.)
  - international perspectives
  - mixed-ability grouping.
  - a wide range of learning strategies.
- Assistance

  Access any assistance you can – parental, teaching assistance, signers, special resources, external support staff and sessions, additional funding, etc. Class teachers and support teachers should work together flexibly to ensure that the children with special needs progress

Application

Inclusive practice: The value of circle time (4–11)

In both the early years and in primary school, circle time is an excellent forum for developing inclusive values and practices.

Many schools use circle time and there seems to be a diversity of aims and approaches to it. The circle may be formed spontaneously when the teacher sees the need or circle time may be timetabled – perhaps weekly or even on a daily basis. There are rules to make circle time discussion work (for example, only speaking when holding an object such as a particular toy or conch shell).

Within the circle, games, discussion and structured activities aim to enhance children's self-esteem, self-knowledge and self-confidence; to develop their communication skills; to provide group participation and experience of democratic problem solving. The circle comes to represent a secure, inclusive place. As Jenny Moseley (the great enthusiast for circle time) has said: 'The circle has always been a symbol of unity, healing and power. Many cultures have roots in the problem-solving, goal-achieving potential of the symbolic circle. (Moseley, J. (1996), *Quality Circle Time in the Primary Classroom* (Wisbech: LDA), p. 70).

Think of the young child's world as a widening circle with the child or self at the core. The circle widens out to include the other person, the world, and finally the realm of values itself. Quality circle time provides a special time in the school week or day when children can think about their relationships and behaviour and during which they can be honest about their problems and feelings. They develop collectively agreed solutions to individual and group problems. They frequently arrive at good solutions. Some teachers link circle time with literacy hour, using poems and stories from literacy hour to prompt the discussion in circle time.

Circles have no top or bottom and they contain rather than exclude.

- Circle time simultaneously promotes:
    - Speaking listening and discussion skills.
    - Democratic values and skills.
    - A forum for democratic decisions.
    - A forum for problem solving.
    - Greater interpersonal understanding between teacher and children and between child and child.
- Circle time resources:
    - Moseley, J. and Sonnett, H. (2005) *Here We Go Round: Quality Circle Time for 3–5 Years Olds* (Trowbridge: Positive Press).
    - Moseley, J. (1996), *Quality Circle Time in the Primary Classroom* (Wisbech: LDA).
    - Leicester, M. (2005), *Stories for Circle Time and Assembly* (London: Routledge).
- Circle time as special time:
    - Quality circle time provides for a special time in the school week (or day) when children can feel part of a group and can correct excluding behaviour.
    - Ideally they will feel sufficiently secure to explore difficult problems and feelings.
    - They can develop collectively agreed solutions to problems such as bullying.
    - They will frequently arrive at good solutions and decisions.

Self-confidence resources

- Plummer, D. (2005), *The Adventures of the Little Tin Tortoise* (London: Jessica Kingsley).
- Plummer, D. (2006), *Self-Esteem Games for Children* (London: Jessica Kingsley).
- Fox, E. (2006), *Classroom Tales Using Storytelling to Build Emotional, Social and Academic Skills Across the Primary Curriculum* (London: Jessica Kingsley).
- Altiero, J. (2006), *No More Stinking Thinking. A Workbook for Teaching Children Positive Thinking* (London: Jessica Kingsley).

Application

Inclusive practice:
The power of story (4–11)

Storytelling has always been a powerful and basic human activity. In all civilizations and cultures, both the activity of storytelling and significant individual stories have been passed down the generations. This is because long before the printed word was available story was the means by which people made sense of their experiences of the world, communicated that understanding and achieved a collective wisdom through passing on accumulated knowledge and values in a memorable and accessible way. Stories add to children's understanding of the complexity and diversity of human motivations and relations, and yet also of the commonality of the human condition. In addition, through story, inclusive learning is fun.

The development of the quality of empathy is intrinsic to the development of story and in particular stories introduce a whole range of values. Moreover, children who develop their love of stories are the children who will develop a love of reading – perhaps the single most powerful educational advantage they can be given.

Children can be encouraged to tell their own stories (for example, 'What I did on my birthday'). They will also be interested to hear about things that have happened to you or to the other children. In addition, children love make-believe stories – adventures, animal stories, stories about a child with whom they can identify, scary stories, realistic stories and fantasy. You can stimulate their imagination by encouraging them to make up a story in some way similar to the one you told.

Stories help us to understand our own experiences and those of others by providing access to inner thoughts and feelings. Thus they readily provide a springboard into greater awareness of inclusive issues such as disability awareness, both at a cognitive level and through deeper empathy at an emotional level. In addition, they implicitly endorse the inclusive values of caring and justice.

Advice

- Used by a good teacher stories can:
  - Stimulate the children's thinking and imagination.
  - Encourage discussion and cooperation.
  - Encourage co-operative learning activities.
  - Review a variety of points of view.
  - Encourage self-knowledge.
  - Teach about the world in which they live.
  - Introduce the complex realm of values.
  - Explore painful emotions and frightening experiences in an enjoyable and safe context.
- Above all the use of story is important in the development of empathy. Narratives not only help to humanize strangers and scapegoats, as, for example, Harriet Beecher Stowe's *Uncle Tom's Cabin* did in the case of white prejudice against black people, but stories also make each one of us sensitive to the particular details of other's pain.
- Stories can simultaneously influence the attitudes of mainstream children and the self-esteem of the 'different' child. Some good story themes for inclusive education would include:
  - alternative lifestyles
  - difference in appearance
  - ethnic diversity; colour and culture
  - disability and impairment
  - hidden disability
  - parental difference.
- Values to look for, which the story will implicitly endorse, include self-esteem, empathy, compassion, co-operation and democracy.
  - To choose good stories ask yourself:
  - Is the material and the language such that it will interest a child of that age and reflect their experiences?
  - Is the story well told? Does it have pace?
  - Is this a good story in literary terms? For example, does it have structure (a definite beginning, middle and end?).
- Are the chapters engaging, believable and inclusive?

Application

Inclusive practice:
The secondary school

In a large secondary school each department needs to develop an inclusive perspective – ethos, policy, curriculum and resources. Clearly the head of department has a key role in terms of encouraging development.

Teachers responsible for the school's support of pupils for whom English is a second language or for disabled pupils will need to work closely with subject teachers.

Some secondary schools have home–school liaison teachers. Their aim should be more than just to do casework with pupils in difficulties. They need time too to help the school develop good home–school links, to set up opportunities to encourage parents into school and to ensure the development of good practice, for example, in the use of appropriate community languages for letters sent to parents/guardians at home.

In developing discipline procedures the elimination of the scope for discrimination should be a consideration. Agreed procedures, universally applicable, help to ensure that no pupil is treated less favourably than any other for no better reason than his or her colour, or impairment or gender, and so on.

Many teachers are still working with stereotyped expectations and children often behave as others expect!

Secondary schools sometime give inadequate career advice and preparation, bearing in mind that girls and pupils from out-groups will face discrimination in the world of work. The placement of black or disabled pupils for community or industrial pre-vocational experience may expose them to racism and disability prejudice. Agencies should be made aware of and asked to support the school's equal opportunity policies and the pupils should be enabled to challenge any discriminatory practices that they encounter. As we know from various reports black youngsters have high expectations of further and higher education but are getting least from it.

Advice

In careers education, teachers should:

- Provide compensatory teaching for ethnic minority and disabled pupils in employability skills and/or knowledge of the labour market.

- Extend the range of role models to which ethnic minority, disabled youngsters and girls have access.

- Extend the range of informal networks to which youngsters have access.

- Prepare ethnic minority pupils and girls and disabled pupils to deal with discrimination they may meet in the labour market (and elsewhere).

- Explore social political issues related to the opportunities open to minority groups of various kinds.

Inclusion in the playground

Some of a child's school experiences take place in the playground. It is important that children are not bullied at playtime and are adequately supervised. Serious assaults (even including loss of life) have taken place at these times.

Racist or other forms of discriminatory incidents, such as verbal abuse, graffiti or physical abuse must never be ignored by the school, whether these occur in the classroom, or, perhaps as is more likely, in the playground.

In a primary school, very young children using racial abuse or other forms of abuse require an educative rather than a punitive response; but in secondary schools such racism should be recognized as a disciplinary matter. Teachers and support staff should know that such abuse is not acceptable and should never be ignored. Procedures for dealing with such incidents should be developed. These procedures need to cover a range of situations. In more serious cases, parents of the abuser and of the abused should be informed.

Racist, sexist or disablist abuse is never justified. Even where a pupil resorting to such abuse was reacting to provocation, the abuse is not an acceptable form of response. Conversely, a black child, for example, reacting to racial abuse, may react inappropriately (for example, with physical violence). This may also require, reprimand, but the teacher should understand the degree of provocation occasioned by racist taunts, and, in any case, should not overlook, and should be seen not to overlook, the original offence (the abuse).

Some LEAs have produced guidelines for their schools about dealing with such incidents. Obviously these should be known by all staff.

Advice

Key points

- Pre-school and primary children need playground supervision for their own safety. Non-inclusive behaviours such as name-calling and abuse should not be ignored but should be dealt with in an educative way.

- In secondary schools, discriminatory behaviours (for example, behaviours such as racial abuse) must be treated as serious disciplinary matters.

- MacDonald, I., Bhavnania, Khan L. and John, C. (1989) give an analysis of a very serious loss of life in the playground of a Manchester school in *Murder in the Playground: Racism and Racial Violence in Manchester Schools* (The MacDonald Report) (London: Limelight Press).

Application

A whole-school approach

Inclusion: The legal context 1

There are several education acts that are relevant to inclusion. For example the Education Act 1981 (incorporating ideas from the Warnlock Report) required that children with special educational needs be educated in ordinary schools, subject to the wishes of parents and provided that this is compatible with receiving the special education they need, with the efficient education of the other children with whom they will be educated, and the efficient use of resources.

There are several pieces of legislation concerning discrimination. The Discrimination Act 1995 introduced measures aimed at ending some of the discrimination experienced by many disabled people. The Sex Discrimination Act 1975 and the Race Relations Act 1976 make discriminations on grounds of race or sex unlawful. Neither pupils nor employees nor anyone else who comes into contact with the education service should be subject to such discrimination. This covers recruitment, promotion, transfer, conditions in employment or dismissal, training, the provision of goods and services, and the education on offer. More recently, we have had the Act Against the Incitement of Religious Hatred.

Advice

Inclusion across all dimensions requires a whole-school approach involving headteachers, staff, parents, pupils and governors. Working together they can create an inclusive school.

Key points

- There are legal requirements relating to equal opportunities in schools.
- Race and sexual discrimination is unlawful.
- The 1981 Education Act contains extensive legislation in the interests of children with special needs.
- The legal context has funding implications. Funding for 'special needs' should be used for the children intended.
- Children with special needs legally require that they have a statement made of those needs:
  - Teachers, parents, doctors and educational psychologists must be involved in the assessment process leading up to the statement.
  - Perhaps partly because parents are legally recognized as having a part to play in this assessment they seem to have been given a genuine inclusion and a voice in the process.
  - Statements are supposed to describe the special needs of the child, the special provision required to meet these and to name the school that will meet them.
  - Many parents have found that although the description of special needs has been made, in fact the school has been unable to meet them. Resource issues have emerged as crucial in the inability of schools to meet statemented special needs. There appears to be a lack of resources preventing the meeting of designated and agreed needs.

Application

Inclusion: The legal context 2

These are important provisions, though ironically they continue to enshrine the notion of 'special needs' (which paves the way for complicated and potentially divisive funding arrangements). True inclusion would be provision appropriate to pupil diversity. That is, provision in common schools, the differentiation of the curriculum, appropriate teacher training, adequate general levels of resources, and a disability aware personal and social education for all.

The Education Act 1988 (ERA) requires schools to have a daily act of worship of a 'broadly Christian' character but allowing scope for multifaith approaches. ERA represents a shifting power from the LEA to schools and school governors.

In 2004 the Children's Act created a framework for local authorities to promote the educational achievement of children in need, including children living in children's homes. It aims to improve universal services to every child and more targeted services for those with additional needs. The act is enabling rather than proscriptive.

- Homosexual equal opportunities in schools are not precluded by Clause 28 or by ERA's Sex Education legislation.
- Children's Act: for consultation on the duty of promoting educational achievement go to www.dfes.gov/consultations.
- Details about the implementation of the Children's Act and the wider reform programme are available in the 2004 publication Every Child Matters: Change for Children (London: HMSO).
- The shifting of power from LEAs to schools may have adverse consequences:
  - If funds are diverted from the special needs for which they are intended.
  - If schools have less access to the kind of specialist advisors LEAs have provided.
  - If schools become so competitive that 'expensive' children, or those 'unhelpful' to the 'league tables' become excluded from mainstream schools of choice.

Application

The school ethos

The school's ethos derives from the dominant values that are embodied in the relationships between people within the school, and with parents and visitors; the visual environment and learning resources; the curriculum and extra-curricular activities; the procedural structures for dealing with decision making, discipline, appointments, staff training, and so on. Obviously the role of the headteacher is a crucial one. Their approach to racial justice and their approach to inclusion will be influential in the school as a whole. Nevertheless, the attitudes and actions of teachers, ancillary staff and governors will also affect the overall ethos. The more people who take inclusion seriously and seek to reflect democratic and humane values within their school, the more nearly that school will obtain the 'whole-school' ideal.

To provide a focus and guide for the whole-school approach, some schools have constructed a policy document. Such documents provide encouragement, support, justification and guidance for worthwhile development in the whole school. The process of constructing such a document is also an educative one and should involve all the school community, so that everyone feels some ownership in it.

In addition to the school policy, the visual environment will reflect the school's inclusion awareness. A good school provides a stimulating visual environment, making extensive use of the pupils' own work, information posters, pictures that are pleasing or relevant to work or activities in progress in the school, and artefacts of all kinds. This visual environment should reflect, positively, our pluralist society. Social out-groups should not be omitted from the visual environment or from the school's library stock.

In short, the atmosphere of the inclusive school is one of respect for all members of the school community, a respect that incorporates respect for difference and diversity, and that respects each person's human rights.

Advice

Resources should reflect an atmosphere of diversity:

- Travel agents and local health authorities may have good posters and leaflets (though avoid images of all white holiday makers with all black waiters!)
- Multicultural services and libraries may provide pictures, books and artefacts
- People are a resource too. Parents and visitors, and representatives from agencies, multicultural resource centres, voluntary organizations, community groups, etc., can add vibrancy and diversity.
- Agencies such as law centres, advice centres and resource centres may offer both resources and speakers to their local schools.

Guidance for schools

The Code of Practice 1994 helps schools to follow good practice in the identification and assessment of special educational needs.

The Organization for Economic Development (OECD) report (1995) – *Integrating Students with Special Needs into Mainstream Schools* – is a useful guide to good practice across the whole school domain.

Many schools have already constructed good policies. These could help to stimulate the thinking of a school that has not already constructed such a policy but wishes to do so

Good schools

Good schools are created when the whole-school community takes responsibility for 'inclusion' in their particular sphere. A 'good citizen' of the school! will contribute to fair and humane practices and have a particular concern for the well-being of the more vulnerable children.

The school assembly

By law, schools must have a collective act of worship. Most schools use their assembly time to reinforce the sense of school community. Assemblies are also practical, being used to convey information. They are also often a significant contribution to the children's spiritual education.

Given this multiplicity of purposes for that special time when the whole school comes together, the school assembly makes an important contribution to the school ethos, and it is also important to the children's (implicit and explicit) values education.

For an inclusive assembly with inclusive values, try to ensure that the children enjoy the occasion and develop a sense of belonging. It helps if different classes can take turns in organizing the assembly with the children making choices about songs, poems and stories. The children could also have a role in leading the assembly or in reading the poem or story. Some of the poems or stories might have been written by the children themselves. Some children might play a musical instrument or (individuals or a group or the school choir) perform a particular hymn or song.

Think of inclusion in relation to all parts of the assembly: from the assembly theme to the tone of the general notices. Consider what values are implicit in the songs/poems/stories that are used.

The school assembly can be a powerful ambassador for inclusion! The general theme could reflect one of the inclusive values (for example justice, love, anti-bullying, respect, sharing, etc.)

- Songs found in commonly used school hymn and song books offer a link into such themes. For example:
  1 *A Better World* (theme: responsible living). No. 60 in *Alleluia* (A&C Black, 1980).
  2 *Working Together* (theme: co-operation around the world). No.37 in *Every Colour Under the Sun* (Ward Lock, 1983).
  3 *Think, Think on These Things* (theme: understanding of others). No. 38 in *Someone's Singing Lord* (A&C Black, 2002).
- Poems commonly used in school anthologies can link into such themes too. For example:
  1 'The Bully' (looks at feelings about being bullied), p. 27 in Moses, B. (ed.) (1998) *Poems About You and Me: A Collection of Poems about Values* (London: Wayland Publishers).
  2 'Friends', in Goldthorpe, M. (2001), *Poems for Circle Time and Literacy Hour* (Wisbech: LDA).
  3 'New Friends', in Goldthorpe, M. (2001), *Poems for Circle Time and Literacy Hour* (Wisbech: LDA).
- The assembly prayer can also reflect the inclusive theme. It can be suitable for a faith school or for a humanistic ethos. For example: assembly theme on kindness and understanding.

Faith school prayer

Heavenly Father,

Help us to be kind and caring to others as you are kind and caring to us and all of your creatures. Bless and guide all those who care for others in the work they do – nurses, doctors, parents, care workers and teachers. Thank you for the wonderful gift of empathy.

Amen.

Prayer for a humanistic or multifaith assembly

Quiet reflection Let us think with gratitude of all those who are kind to us (pause). Let us think now, of ways we can be kind to our family and our friends today (pause). Let us reflect on why it is good to be a human being and to have emotions (pause).

The head or senior management

The biggest single influence on the ethos and learning in schools is that of the headteacher – and in secondary schools, the senior management team. Inclusive management will be democratic management, promoting democratic structures and values in the aims, consultation practices, decision-making processes, administrative routines, curriculum implementation, teaching and learning methods, staff appointments, record keeping and student assessment. A democratic approach ensures everyone can feel part of a just community.

It is important that the headteacher involves colleagues, and, where appropriate, pupils and parents and governors, not just in formulating the school policy, but in subsequent decisions and developments. For example, the head teacher should consult his staff about what issues ought to involve parental consultation. As many parents as possible should be involved and parental views genuinely reflected in decisions.

The language of consultation must not hinder communication. Therefore, languages of different communities may need to be used. The head should also seek to avoid bureaucratic language and acronyms that may not be familiar.

Inclusive management will be mindful that the staff of the school include the ancillary staff. For example, INSET will include all staff, as will non-discriminatory interview procedures and promotion policies.

The role that the head takes in supporting professional development is crucial. There is a vast literature on styles of leadership but essentially, democratic leaders who demonstrate a commitment to the continuing professional development of their staff are most likely to empower their teachers.

Headteachers are increasingly having to meet increasing demands in a complex system. They are expected to be entrepreneurs with vision and unlimited energy and effective management skills. They deserve support from colleagues, governors and LEA, and their own professional development has never been of greater importance.

Advice

Inclusion in the management task areas:

1 Managing the overall policy:
the aims and objectives of the school; long-terms plans; school leadership/management styles; standards; management of time; management of change.

2 Managing school communications and decision-making structures:
methods of consultation; provision of information; communications between staff; resolution of conflict; handling meetings; decision making; problem solving; team work; administration forms; staff handbook.

3 Managing the curriculum:
devise a new curriculum policy; curriculum implementation; development and evaluation; teaching and learning methods; subject areas; timetables; a fair examination; homework policy; other arrangements.

4 Managing staff:
maintaining effective relationships for teaching and non-teaching staff; staff appointments; job descriptions; pastoral care of staff; motivation; staff development needs, reviews and provision; advice; role of staff with responsibilities; in-service training; teacher loads; probationers; student teachers; coping with stress.

5 Managing pupils:
arrangements for groupings, testing and assessment; pastoral care; record keeping; discipline; continuity of education; special needs; social and personal development of all.

6 Managing material and resources:
buildings, equipment, furniture, materials; finance, resource allocation; assessing needs; health and safety.

7 Managing external relations:
working with governors, LEA; relating to parents, the local community; involvement of parents and governors in schools; inter-school liaison; links with commerce and industry; media; support services.

8 Managing the process of monitoring and evaluating the school:
assessment of all aspects of school life and its effect on all pupils and groups of pupils.

Application

Staffing and inclusion

Much of what we explained in relation to the curriculum, to teaching approaches, to resources, etc. was mainly directed at teachers. However, training should include ancillary staff. All staff should receive a high level of training in inclusion issues and awareness. All staff should also experience non-discriminatory and respectful treatment. Teachers and ancillary staff should work flexibly together for the good of pupils – in a democratic, non-hierarchical atmosphere. In other words, everyone should be appreciated for their contributions as a valued, full member of the school community.

There tends to be fewer disabled staff in schools, or staff from minority ethnic groups. The higher up the hierarchy, the more obvious this absence. (The majority of primary school teachers are women, for example, and yet a disproportionate number of primary headteachers are men.) It is important to ensure that there is no unintentional or indirect discrimination in recruitment procedures.

Considering the value, for the children, of diversity in the role models they experience of people in positions of authority, there may even be a case for positive action. It is not against the discrimination laws, for example, to encourage applicants from members of minority groups by ensuring that your information about vacancies reaches into all sections of the community, and by stating that you are an equal opportunity employer, or, indeed, require someone with equal opportunity expertise or special needs/cultural diversity experience and expertise.

An inclusive staffing checklist:

- Do the school staff represent a diversity of background?
- Are women, black teachers and disabled staff employed only in the ancillary sector or on the teaching staff but only on the lower grades?
- Do only teaching staff have expertise in relation to inclusive education – to cultural diversity, to special needs, to gender issues?
- Do you consider these kinds of expertise deficiencies when recruiting for new staff?
- When you interview staff for appointment or promotion, do you include governors who represent equal opportunity interests, commitment or experience?
- How democratic, inclusive and respectful is the school in its treatment of ancillary staff?
- How well do teachers and support staff work together?
- Do any of the above need further development?

Application

Parents and inclusion

Inclusive schools work with pupils' parents, recognizing that the education of children requires a partnership between home and schools. Some multi-ethnic schools have home–school liaison teachers and multicultural education has encouraged parental involvement, emphasizing the importance of dialogue between parents and teachers and also the need for consultation of parents about educational matters. Similarly, the issue of statementing for the 'special needs' of disabled children has also encouraged more partnerships between parents and schools.

Obviously language barriers should not be permitted to either hinder communication or consultation and parents who do not speak English should be catered for – through translation of letters home and through the provision of interpreters on key occasions. Teachers and headteachers could also try to avoid bureaucratic language. In keeping with the democratic values of inclusion, consultation should include some parental involvement in decision making so that parents are genuinely part of education and developments affecting their children.

The 1986 Act requires governors to produce a report for parents. The law requires governors to say when and where the annual parents' meeting is to take place, at which the report will be discussed. Obviously, governors should choose a time and place convenient to most parents and should try to establish a friendly atmosphere. Perhaps refreshments could be provided. The meeting is a good opportunity to consult, as well as to report to parents, and should be an opportunity to discuss issues on matters of concern. The meeting should remind governors that they are accountable to the parents.

The law requires that the report gives the names of all the governors, including the parent governors, and explain the arrangement for the next election of parent governors. The report must also say how the school is developing links with the community and describe the school curriculum.

Advice

Key points

The governor's report to parents should:

- Name the governors and the parent governors.
- Explain the arrangements for electing the next parent governors.
- Give information about funding.
- Give information about examination and test results.
- Give information about how the school is developing links with the community.
- Give information about the curriculum.
- The law requires that the report be produced in languages other then English, if this is worthwhile.
- The report should avoid bureaucratic language, professional jargon and acronyms.
- The report must be sent to all parents not less than two weeks before the meeting.
- The report should reflect inclusive values and the school's commitment to equal opportunities.

Application

School governors and inclusion

Governors, too, need to have a commitment to inclusion. Training in, and an understanding of, equal opportunity legislation and policies is desirable. The Education Reform Act 1986 and 1988 greatly increased the responsibilities of school governing bodies. Duties include local financial management, staffing and appointing of staff, grievance and dismissals, school meals, ensuring that the national curriculum is taught and providing an annual report to, and meeting with, parents.

Non-statutory tasks commonly undertaken by governors include liaison and consultation with teachers, parents and the local community and general advice and support to the headteacher, who has the day-to-day responsibility for running the school. Since governors are responsible for hiring and firing staff they need to understand how to avoid discrimination in developing advertising, interviewing and selection procedures that are genuinely free of race, gender and disability bias.

Ideally, the composition of the governing body should itself be representative of the local community and, indeed, of the society as a whole – the society in which their pupils will one day find employment and take their place as adult citizens. Yet there are few black governors, few female chairpersons, few disabled governors and most have been drawn from the professional and managerial classes. A more diverse governing body draws on a wider range of experience, awareness and expertise. Many governors are co-opted. Could a more diverse and inclusive group be co-opted?

Governors need to raise the issue of inclusion and devise a development plan that includes monitoring the development.

The school governors should address these questions:

- How will equal opportunities be considered regularly in governor meetings? It should figure in some form on every agenda. The pattern should be decided at the planning stage – will equal opportunities be a general item at each meeting, or will this be sub-divided for separate discussion at separate meetings (class, race, gender, etc.)?

- Will special needs in the school be considered at every meeting?

- Will teaching staff who are invited to contribute to the curriculum slot on each agenda be asked in advance to include consideration of inclusive curricular development in their field?

- What can governors do to ensure a whole-school approach to inclusion?

- Has the school got an equal opportunity/inclusion policy statement yet, for example? If not, how is this to be constructed? How will governors ensure wide consultation and the involvement of pupils, parents, teaching and ancillary staff?

- What training have governors and staff received in inclusion/equal opportunities?

- What more could be done? Could a whole-school INSET day be arranged, involving governors and non-teaching staff too?

- What about the school ethos? Is this conducive to the promotion of equal opportunities and inclusive values? If not, how should it be changed, and how will these changes be implemented?

Five key governor duties and inclusion

Each of the five main governing body duties and powers has an inclusion dimension:

- Local financial management

  The budget for special educational needs, for cultural diversity resources or language support in city schools should be as generous as possible. Particularly in working-class areas, the budget for examination fees should not be so tight that the school is tempted to discourage pupils who teachers think are not certain to pass. The budget for special educational needs should be as generous a possible, because meeting special needs is often expensive.

- Staffing

  Consider equal opportunity procedures in recruitment and promotion. In addition, consider whether the teaching staff have sufficient expertise across the inclusion issues: cultural diversity; special needs; gender issues, etc. If not, bear this in mind during recruitment of new staff.

- The curriculum

  Take an informed interest in the school curriculum and show interest and commitment in inclusive curriculum development. It is important that the staff know of the governors' commitment to inclusion. Governors should ensure that the National Curriculum is permeated with an inclusive perspective.

- Discipline

  Governors should seek to avoid stereotyping and be humane and fair within an expectation of good behaviour.

- The governors' report and parents meeting

  As was discussed, the law requires governors to hold this meeting and presents a good opportunity to involve parents in the school's inclusive practice development and values.

Advice

Resources for governors

- The following resources help governing bodies with their planning and implementation of inclusive practice:

  The DfES. A full list of DfES and Her Majesty's Inspectorate (HMI) publications is available free of charge from: Publications Dispatch Centre, Cannon Park, Honeypot Lane, Stanmore, Middlesex, HA7 1AZ.

  DSEE material includes circulars on special needs, on religious education and collective worship, on sex education on curriculum matters and on special needs: gender and ethnicity.

- The LEA may have specialist advisors or resource centres. Find out what advice, resources and checklists are available both locally and nationally.

- Not all developments require additional funding so much as a re-orientation in approach. For example, expenditure on books should be based on selection guided by inclusion criteria.

School resources

- Governors could consider building up a small library of handbooks, checklists and relevant books for the use of staff and governors.

Further reading

- Wragg, T. and Partington, J. A. (1981), *A Handbook for School Governors* (London: Routledge).

Continuing professional development and inclusion

Professional development

- Learning is a lifelong matter, and consonant with this, professional development does not finish with the end of initial training, but continues across a teacher's whole career.

- Professional development is not merely about obtaining mechanical competencies and a stock of subject knowledge to be passed on to one's pupils. Good professional development involves acquiring a much deeper understanding about the social and values context in which teaching takes place and about the crucial importance of reflective teachers for quality learning in progressively improving schools.

Lifelong learning

The pace of change in modern industrial democracies has given impetus to the lifelong learning movement. Modern societies are becoming better organized to provide learning opportunities throughout life for professional updating, personal development, political awareness and good citizenship.

Continuous professional development

Teachers' continuing professional development has a key role in such learning societies; teachers need to be reflective practitioners who continuously reflect on their own teaching in order to improve it and to be open to new perspectives and approaches.

They need to have an ongoing commitment to their own professional updating, personal development and political awareness, and to equip their pupils to become lifelong learners – enjoying learning and knowing how to learn.

Advice

Continuous professional development

- Professional development implies a high level of training and involves ongoing learning.
- Professional development implies initiation into inclusive values and fair standards of conduct.
- The pace of change in the modern world means that professionals need to update their skills on a regular basis, including ongoing development for meeting the special needs of students with a variety of impairments.
- Teachers' professional development is essential for maintaining inclusive teaching in schools. These moral demands on teachers require development of a high order.

A reflective teacher with sharpened inclusive awareness will:

- Identify and challenge unfair or biased assumptions. Such a teacher will question and challenge passively accepted traditions and routines that are unintentionally discriminatory.
- Challenge the importance of context. Such a teacher develops awareness of relating our thinking to the context in which it is set and therefore recognizes the development required for cultural pluralism.
- Imagine and explore alternatives. Creative teachers think beyond the obvious and immediately logical and are able therefore to adopt differing perspectives and standpoints.
- Develop reflective scepticism. Such a teacher is wary of claims to universal truths or absolutes. Because others think differently than we do does not mean that either of us is right. Sometimes there is no right or wrong answer but rather a variety of valid approaches. There may be no one 'proper' approach.

Further reading

Day, C. (1999), *Developing Teachers: The Challenges of Lifelong Learning* (London: Routledge).

Field, J. and Leicester, M. (2000) *Lifelong Learning: Education Across the Lifespan* (London: Routledge).

Application

Raising awareness:
Training for inclusion

An awareness of inclusion issues and values, of equal opportunity policies and practices, of cultural diversity, of meeting special needs, of the gender and sexuality issues, should permeate the school curriculum and ethos. School structures and routines should follow sound anti-discriminatory guidelines. However, in addition to this general re-orientation of perspective, this impregnation of an inclusive dimension, there is also a need to provide all staff with more specific understandings of the functioning and the nature of inequalities of social groups. Such specific understanding would include:

- knowledge of our colonial history
- background information about impairment
- knowledge about statementing
- understanding of the experiences of minority groups
- the nature of prejudice
- the nature of institutional discrimination
- knowledge and understanding of other cultural traditions
- understanding of stereotyping
- understanding of ethnocentricity
- understanding of language issues (English as a second language (E2L) dialect, mother tongue provision)
- understanding of the social model of disability
- understanding of disability as a form of oppression.

The starting point is to ensure that staff have received awareness-raising education – in other words, experiential learning about racism, disability awareness, sexism and homophobia. Once awareness has been sharpened, there is a re-orientation in perspective and an openness to recognizing and changing one's own prejudices, and a commitment to ending such prejudice and discrimination in and through education.

Advice

- Consider devoting a staff training day to inclusion awareness.
- All staff (teaching and ancillary) and governors should be invited.
- The topics covered will suit the particular school but should aim to be experiential and participatory – exercises and discussions rather than lectures!
- The programme should cover three main areas:
  - Understanding discrimination and inequality in all its dimensions: through exercises, discussion, videos, etc., explore the concepts of prejudice in its many forms and the functioning of stereotypes in the media and in education and the relationship between prejudice and discrimination.
  - The nature of change in schools and how to facilitate this: explore, discuss and agree on where changes and developments are most needed and how to set up an appropriate working group or to designate appropriate responsibilities, etc., in order to effectively achieve the desired change.
  - The practical implications for school practice (structures, governance, relationships, ethos, curriculum): brainstorm any practical steps that could and should be taken in the various domains. Set up realistic goals for short, medium and long-term achievement.
- Handouts and other resources used to stimulate discussion, etc., should be of a good professional standard.
- Incorporate displays of inclusive learning resources: books, posters, objects, etc. The aim is learning and supporting, etc., not preaching or judging.
- Of course only so much can be achieved in one day. However, it is amazing how much learning and awareness can be generated by good experiential sessions and well-structured discussion. The day is meant to be only the start of continuous awareness and learning – the start of an awareness journey.

Application

Further reading

Allport, W. H. (1958), *Prejudice* (New York. Doubleday).

Altiero, J. (2006), *No More Stinking Thinking. A Workbook for Teaching Children Positive Thinking* (London: Jessica Kingsley).

Arnot, M. (ed.) (1985), *Race and Gender Equal Opportunities Policies in Education*, (Oxford: Pergamon)

Baker, K. and Smith, B. (2006), *Making a Spectacle of Bullying* (London: Sage).

Brandling, Redvers and Cass-Beggs, Barbara (1983), *Every Colour Under the Sun* (Sussex, UK: Ward Lock).

Bridges, R. (1999), *Through My Eyes* (London: Scholastic).

Canadian Cultural Society of the Deaf (2007), *The Smart Princess and Other Deaf Tales* (Canada: Second Story Press).

Circle of Inclusion Project (2002), *Guide for Reviewing Children's Literature that Include People with Disabilities: Books Written for Children Three to Five Years of Age*, compiled by Diane Nastir.

Clough, P. and Corbett, J. (2000), *Theories of Inclusive Education*, (London: Sage).

Cole, M. (ed.) (1989), *The Social Context of Schooling*, (London: The Falmer Press).

Cotterill, P. *et al.* (eds) (2007), *Challenges and Negotiations for Women in Higher Education* (Dordrecht: Springer).

Day, C. (1999), *Developing Teachers: The Challenges of Lifelong Learning* (London: Routledge).

Delacre, L. (1996), *Golden Tales: Myths, Legends and Folktales from Latin America* (London: Scholastic).

DFEE (1998), *'The Learning Age: A Renaissance for a New Britain'*, www.lifelonglearning.dfee.gov.uk/greenpaper/index.htm

Doyle, J. L. and Wells, S. (1997), 'Social Class and the Effective School Paradigm', in *International Journal of Educational Management*, 11, 4.

Dubin, N. (2006), *Being Bullied: Strategies and Solutions for People with Asperger's Syndrome* (London: Jessica Kingsley).

Field, J. and Leicester, M. (2000), *Lifelong Learning: Education Across the Lifespan* (London: Routledge).

Fox, E. (2006), *Classroom Tales Using Storytelling to Build Emotional, Social and Academic Skills Across the Primary Curriculum* (London: Jessica Kingsley).

Fryer, P. (1984), *Staying Power: History of Black People in Britain* (London. Pluto Press).

Gadsby, David and Hoggarth, John (1980), *Alleluia* (London: A&C Black).

Gaine, C. (1987), *No Problem Here: A Practical Approach to Education and 'Race' in White Schools* (London. Hutchinson).

Goldthorpe, M. (2001), *Poems for Circle Time and Literacy Hour* (Wisbech: LDA).

Harrop, B. (ed.) (2002), *Someone's Singing Lord* (London: A&C Black).

Hausherr, R. (1997), *Celebrating Families* (London: Scholastic).

Heo, Y. (1994), *One Afternoon* (London: Orchard).

Hicks, D. (1981), *Minorities* (London and Oxford: Heinemann).

Hull, J. (1992), *Touching the Rock: An Experience of Blindness* (London: Vintage).

ILEA, (1986), *Positive Images*

Jackson, L. (2002), *Freaks, Geeks and Asperger Syndrome: A User Guide to Adolescence* (London: Jessica Kingsley).

King, C. and Barret, L. (1997), *Oh, Freedom! Kids Talk About the Civil Rights Movement with the People Who Made it Happen* (London: Knopf).

Kupper, Lisa, (ed.) (2001), *Children's Literature and Disability* (National Information Centre for Children and Youth with Disabilities (NICHCY)).

Leicester, M. (1993), *Race for a Change in Continuing and Higher Education* (Buckingham: Open University Press).

Leicester, M. (1998), *Disability Voice. Towards an Enabling Education* (London: Jessica Kingsley).

Leicester, M. (2005), *Stories for Circle Time and Assembly* (London: Routledge).

Leicester, M. (2007), *Early Years Stories for the Foundation Stage* (London: Routledge).

Leicester, M. (2007), *Special Stories for Disability Awareness. Stories and Activities for Teachers, Parents and Professionals* (London: Jessica Kingsley).

Leicester, M. and Johnson, G. (2004), *Stories for Inclusive Schools. Developing Young Pupils' Skills* (London: Routeledge Falmer).

Milner, D. (1983), *Children and Race Ten Years On* (London. Ward Lock).

Morpurgo , Michael (2004), *Private Peaceful* (New York: HarperCollins).

Moseley, J. (1996), *Helping Children Deal with Bullying, Anger and Conflict* (Wisbech: LDA).

Moseley, J. (1996), *Quality Circle Time in the Primary Classroom* (Wisbech: LDA)

Moseley, J. (1996), *Working Towards a Whole School Policy on Self-Esteem and Positive Behaviour* (Wisbech: LDA).

Moseley, J. and Sonnett, H. (2005), *Here We Go Round: Quality Circle Time for 3–5 Years Old*s (Trowbridge: Positive Press).

Moses, B. (ed.) (1998), *Poems About You and Me: A Collection of Poems about Values* (London: Wayland Publishers).

Pinkney, S. L. (2000), *Shades of Black: A Celebration of Our Children* (London: Scholastic).

Plummer, D. (2005), *The Adventures of the Little Tin Tortoise* (London: Jessica Kingsley).

Plummer, D. (2006), *Self-Esteem Games for Children* (London: Jessica Kingsley).

Richardson, R. (1990), *Daring to be a Teacher*, (: Trentham Books).

Rigby, K. (2002), *Stop The Bullying: A Handbook for Schools* (London: Jessica Kingsley).

Serrailler, I (2003), *The Silver Sword* (New York: Red Fox).

Stones, R. (1983), *"Pore Out the Coco Janet" Sexism in Children's Books*, (London: Longman).

Swain, J. et al. (eds) (2002), *Disabling Barriers, Enabling Environments* (London: Sage).

Swann Report, (1985), *Education for All* (London: HMSO).

Tarpley, N. A. (1998), *I Love My Hair!* (London: Little, Brown).

Taylor, M. D. (1999), *Roll of Thunder, Hear My Cry* (London: Scholastic).

The MacDonald Report *Murder in the Playground: Racism and Racial Violence in Manchester Schools* (London: Limelight Press).

The Organization for Economic Development (OECD) report (1995) – *Integrating Students with Special Needs into Mainstream Schools*

Thomas, J. C. (1999), *You Are My Perfect Baby* (London: Harper Collins).

Warnock, M (1988), *Report of the Committee of Enquiry into the Education of Handicapped Children and Young People* (London: HMSO).

Weiss, G. D. and Thiele, B. (1995), *What a Wonderful World* (London: Atheneum).

Weston, Molly (ed) (2002), *Diversity in Children's Lives: Children's Books and Classroom Helps* (Chapel Hill, The University of North Carolina, FPG Child Development Institute, PFL).

Wragg, T. and Partington, J.A. (1981), *A Handbook for School Governors*, (London: Routledge).